Tokens of Grace

Cape Breton's Open-Air Communion Tradition

Laurie Stanley-Blackwell

Cape Breton University Press Inc.
Sydney, Nova Scotia

Cape Breton University Press recognizes the support of the Province of Nova Scotia, through the Department of Tourism, Culture and Heritage. We are pleased to work in partnership with the Culture Division to develop and promote our cultural resources for Nova Scotians.

NOVA SCOTIA
Tourism, Culture and Heritage

Cover Design: Cathy MacLean, Pleasant Bay, NS
Layout: Mike Hunter, Louisbourg, NS
Printing by Kromar Printing Ltd., Winnipeg, MB

Library and Archives Canada Cataloguing in Publication
Stanley-Blackwell, Laurie C. C
    Tokens of grace : Cape Breton's open-air communion tradition / Laurie Stanley-Blackwell.

Includes bibliographical references.
ISBN-13: 978-1-897009-18-5
ISBN-10: 1-897009-18-6

    1. Presbyterian Church--Nova Scotia--Cape Breton Island--Customs and
practices--History. 2. Lord's Supper. 3. Religious gatherings--Nova Scotia--Cape Breton Island--History. 4. Scots--Nova Scotia--Cape Breton Island--Religion--History. 5. Cape Breton Island (N.S.)--Church history. I. Title.

BX9002.C36S74 2006   285'.271695   C2006-906234-X

Cape Breton University Press
PO Box 5300
Sydney, NS B1P 6L2 Canada

To my mother, who was such a delightful travel companion on my first research pilgrimage to Cape Breton during the spring of 1979.

This book is but a token of a greater gratitude.

Contents

Acknowledgements

Little did I anticipate that when I first started studying the history of Cape Breton Presbyterianism for my MA thesis in 1978, I would find it such an engrossing subject that would continue to command my attention for almost thirty years. As my research progressed and the story unfolded, I became acquainted with a remarkable cast of historical figures, many of them larger than life, such as the spirited Isabella Gordon MacKay and the fearsome, God-fearing Rev. Norman McLeod. There was nothing anemic about Cape Breton's early Presbyterian church and its people who were products of a vivid history and culture. Their most striking hallmark was their strong faith. For them, religion was not consigned to the periphery of everyday life; it left a deep imprint on their psyche, anchoring their identity, infusing them with a sense of community, filtering their world views and shaping their hearts and minds. For these staunch believers, few rituals were as important as the open-air communion which became a central landmark in their spiritual and social lives. This sacramental event, with its feast of sermons and harvest of souls, was transported from Scotland to Cape Breton in the early 19th century with little dilution. It retained, against all odds, many of its original characteristics for almost three-quarters of a century, an event sacred, social and wonderfully human on all levels. By the early 20th century, Cape Breton's open-air communion was only a shadow of its former self, increasingly at odds with the changing spirit of the times. Among the Island's Presbyterian people, this tradition too would go the way of homespun, to be regarded as a nostalgic relic of remembrance.

For the historian, the study of this tradition offers many fruitful paths of inquiry, beckoning one into such fields of investigation as religion, foodways, gender, rituals, dress behaviour and material culture. Regrettably, there are few people alive today in Cape Breton who can recall first-hand these joyous occasions. Their voices have faltered and faded, and the "rivers of memory" will soon be little more than traces in the dust. It is hoped that the following study recaptures some of the vitality of this tradition both in its heyday and its retreat.

In the writing of this monograph, I have incurred many debts of gratitude. I wish to acknowledge the assistance of the following people: Clayton Bartlett, Winnifred Bean, Ona Bjornson, Irving H. Blifford, Ron Caplan, Hugh Cameron, Irene Castagliola (*Harper's Magazine*), Judith Colwell (Maritime Conference Archives), Anne Connell (Beaton Institute, Cape Breton University), Mike Dolmont, Carolyn Earle, Betty Fownes, Jocelyn Gillis (Antigonish Heritage Museum), Marie T. Gillis, Whitman Gillis, Evie Grew, Kathryn Hilder, Shirley Horne, Muriel Kaiser, Rev. Robert Lyle, Catherine MacAskill, Norma MacAdam, Mervyn MacAulay, Annie MacAulay, Jean MacAulay, Bernice MacDonald, Charles H. MacDonald, Kay MacDonald, Rev. Ewen MacDougall, Sadie MacInnis, Dolly MacKay, Prof. A. A. MacKenzie, Rev. Angus MacKinnon, Jennifer MacKinnon, Jessie MacLean, Rev. Neil J. McLean, Dr. Jean MacLennan, Annie MacLeod, Dollie B. MacLeod, Donald Macleod, Eveline MacLeod, John MacLeod (Nova Scotia Archives and Records Management), Karen MacLeod (New Glasgow Public Library), Robert McLeod, Annie MacMillan, Clara MacMillan, Flora MacMillan, Marion MacNeil, Anne Marie MacPherson, Very Rev. Angus MacQueen, Charles

MacVicar, Dr. Robert Morgan, Bill Morrison, Donald N. Morrison, Jessie Morrison, Martha Murray, Father Bernie O'Connor, Nelena Patterson, Catherine Poole, Dorothy Pottie, Rev. Dr. Cecil H. Rose, Catherine Ross, Jim St. Clair, Dr. Leigh Schmidt, Alexander Smith, Evelyn Smith, Karen Smith (Special Collections, Dalhousie University), Drs. George and Ruth Stanley, Norma Strickland, Enid L. Stuart and Hazel Trask. Special acknowledgement should also be given to Marjorie Jeans who cheerfully tracked down leads for me, and to the Rev. Donald Sutherland and Rev. Ritchie Robinson who introduced me to a network of knowledgeable interviewees who shared memories and hospitality in generous measure. I also appreciate the invaluable assistance of Mary Jane Lamond who provided English translations for some of my Gaelic sources and Shamus MacDonald who shared his expertise as an interviewer and translator. I am also indebted to Effie Rankin who kindly responded to a flurry of last-minute queries about correct Gaelic usage and to Michael Linkletter whose proficiency in Gaelic proved most helpful. As well, I would like to extend thanks to my husband, John Blackwell, for his editorial acumen, to my family for their gallant support and to Cape Breton University Press and its editor, Mike Hunter, for ably guiding this monograph to publication. Finally, the research funding of the Centre for Regional Studies, St. Francis Xavier University, is gratefully noted.

Laurie Stanley-Blackwell
Loch Mór House
21 August 2006

We proceeded on horseback at half-past ten in the forenoon, under heavy rain, and found the roads literally covered with groups of people, who, although drenched to the skin, were hastening to the place. Every opening in the wood poured out hundreds. The Bras d'Or was covered with boats, some from West Bay, some from Malagawarch [sic] and Hagomah [sic], some from Bedeque & c., distance varying from forty to ten miles—as I passed along I thought with myself what would the people of Edinburgh, who consider it an intolerable hard-ship to walk a quarter of a mile to church in such a day—What would they say, were they to witness the scene?

Hugh McLeod, Boularderie Communion, 1851
The Missionary Record and Ecclesiastical Intelligencer of the Free Church of Nova Scotia (1852) 158-159.

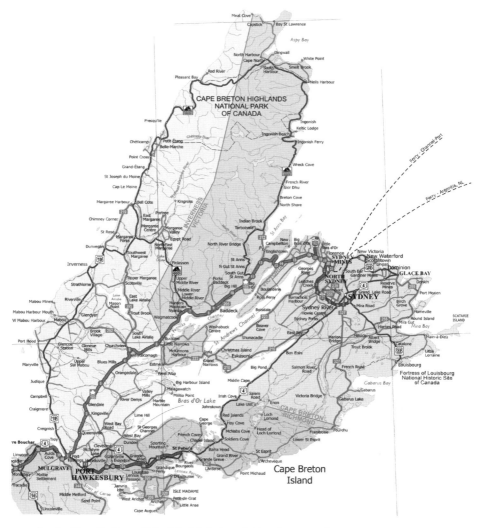

Chapter One

From Scotland to Cape Breton

On August 1, 1858, William Jardine of Little Pond in Little Bras d'Or greeted the Sabbath day writing these words in his journal: "...a few Sabbaths more has [*sic*] to pass away, before the sacrament of the Lord's Supper is to be dispensed at Sydney Mines, and let it be the Lord's will for me to see that day, and to take my seat at his table."[1] This was no ordinary event that Jardine awaited with such anticipation. For weeks before and after the communion, the diary of this farmer and Presbyterian elder overflowed with meditations about his spiritual state and his keen desire to foretaste the joys of heaven. Between 1840 and 1890, the so-called "sacramental season"—the Sàcramaid—was a dominant symbol in the lives of Cape Breton's Presbyterians. It was both the social event and spiritual highlight of the year, a time when people engaged in prayer, fellowship and renewal, as well as feasting and courtship.

In 18th- and 19th-century Scotland, the annual five-day open-air communion was a vital part of Scottish Presbyterian culture. Once a year, usually after the summer shearing or the fall harvest, men and women gathered to celebrate the sacramental season. During the religiously vibrant 1830s, these meetings, attended by vast concourses of individuals numbering between six and fifteen thousand, were an effective means of exciting the pious fervour of the Highland

Scots.[2] Whole communities, even regions, converged for this great religious occasion, arriving in carts, buggies and on foot. As the *Ross-shire Journal* exclaimed: "No gathering in the Highlands—funerals excepted—so strongly impresses a stranger as this outdoor meeting."[3] One eyewitness later recalled with extraordinary vividness seeing the streams of celebrants from the shires of Ross, Cromarty, Inverness and even Sutherland, who gathered at the burn of Ferintosh, arriving in their carts, buggies and on foot: "pedestrians of both sexes, travelling in groups of three or four; these last occupied almost invariably conversing upon some Scripture text or giving notes of the various sermons they had heard."[4] The arrival of parishioners from adjacent congregations was preceded by the animated preparation by the hosting householders of bannock, salt fish and potatoes and arrangements for makeshift sleeping quarters in barns and attics. With high expectations, the parishioners assembled in the fields, the matrons in mutch caps, the elderly in grey-blue cloaks pulled around their heads and the young women bareheaded, awaiting with rapt attention the preacher's inspiring message.

This annual celebratory gathering and its pageant of pilgrims represented a grand evocation of faith and community. These poignant scenes were much more than an historical curiosity. They were an elaborate composite of cultural meanings, religious beliefs and social relations set against a backdrop of heated theological discourse. The Lord's Supper, to borrow the terminology of the cultural anthropologist Clifford Geertz, is a prime example of "a paradigmatic human event."[5] On its most mundane level, this central ritual for the Christian community is a symbolic re-enactment of the most basic of human activities, that is, eating and drinking. On a deeper, more complex level, it represents an extraordinary meal, a form of spiritual nourishment that rises above everyday life and represents the highest expression of the individual and collective encounter between God and His believers and the human journey to salvation.

14

From its inception as a Protestant denomination, the Presbyterian Church always laid more emphasis on prayers and sermons than upon the administration of the sacraments. This does not mean that the sacraments, such as Holy Communion, were disregarded and devalued. On the contrary, this sacrament was deemed an important ceremonial observance. In sum, it represented a solemn act, a seal of grace already given, and a "renewed consecration" to Christian service.[6] But it was not regarded by Presbyterians, as it was by Roman Catholics or Anglicans, as the Eucharistic sacrifice. Among the intellectual triad of the Protestant Reformation— Ulrich Zwingli, John Calvin and Martin Luther—there was little interpretive consensus on the nature and role of the Lord's Supper. All three camps took a dogmatic stand on such fundamental issues as meaning, frequency and eligibility. Calvin, whose teachings were foundational to the development of the Scottish Presbyterian Church, tended to occupy the middle ground, especially on the matter of communion. Unlike Zwingli, Calvin viewed the Lord's Supper as far more than just a collective act of historical remembrance and commemoration. For him, it was a stimulus to faith and devotion, a token rather than a channel of divine grace, which solidified the bonds between the real presence of the Risen Christ and communicants. Although he dismissed transubstantiation as a popish fiction, Calvin cautioned believers against taking the Lord's Supper lightly, without an exhaustive preparatory self-examination. On the issue of how frequently this ordinance should be administered, Calvin also took a firm doctrinal posture. Communion, he contended, should be celebrated regularly as an integral part of every worship service. For Zwingli, such a notion was anathema, far too Roman Catholic for his tastes.

This Reformation legacy of schism and ambiguity shaped the complexion of the theology and practice of the Lord's Supper in Scotland. Here, the Presbyterian communion had a convoluted, even turbulent past.[7] It was the impassioned Calvinist, John Knox, who transplanted the basis tenets of the Reformation to Scotland, where he laboured to purge the sacramental ritual of its Catholic trappings; few things filled him with more horror than the "stinking and filthy masse" with its emphasis on "adoration and priestly sacrifice."[8] During the second half of the 16th century, the spread of Scottish Protestantism under the bold defenders of the Scottish church, its own ranks fraught with schism, was no easy victory. Still, this period was one of sowing and reaping. Many of the distinctive features of the Presbyterian communion were implemented at this time. According to historian Leigh Schmidt,"Such things as preparatory services, sitting to receive the elements, self-examination, careful fencing of the tables and communion tokens were all evident in one form or another from the early years of the Reformation in Scotland."[9] Similarly, the open-air communion became a potent spiritual force by the 1630s and "braved the religious unrest and civil war that followed."[10] As the Presbyterian cause gained momentum in the southwest of Scotland and was further solidified by the drafting of a National Covenant in 1638, episcopal and royal forces mounted a formidable repression that grew more militant and gory by the 1670s and 1680s. Under the boot of both mitre and crown, the so-called Covenanters met in open defiance, gathering in private houses, barns and even vast outdoor assemblies, despite draconian laws that deemed attendance by 1670 at such gatherings treasonable and preaching at them a capital offence. Threats of fines, banishment, imprisonment and even execution did little to crush their spirit of rebellion—in fact, these deterrents spurred them on. According to John Blackader's memoirs, an outdoor communion at Colmonell in Ayrshire in 1679 drew a substantial following: "there were many min[iste]rs there, much preaching, the greatest Multitude that ever I heard was on the fields in Scotland, before or since."[11] The spectacle of defiance and subversion served two essential purposes; it was a vehicle for both protest and religious fervour. Hounded and harried, the Covenanters became the stuff of legends. These stories of persecution, suffering and sacrifice would be prized by their Presbyterian heirs, feeding their sense of pride and furnishing them with a constellation of martyrs who contributed to an almost halo-like glow over the early history of the Scottish church.

The "Glorious Revolution" of 1688-1689 signalled the triumph of the Presbyterian Church in Scotland and the vindication of their doctrine and forms of worship, but did not close the chapter on the much debated format of the open-air communion. According to Thomas Burns, there was "great irregularity" in the ministration of the Lord's Supper in Scotland in the years following the "Glorious Revolution."[12] With neither uniform dates nor fixed intervals for their observances, communions were prolonged over two or even three successive Sundays. In some of the more populous centres, there were two distinct communions held before noontime, the first service frequently starting before daybreak; in Glasgow and Stirling, services began as early as 4 o'clock.[13] As late as the 18th century, there were many instances of a communion not being held for five, ten or even more years.[14] One extreme example was Shapinsay, Orkney, where the Lord's Supper was administered only once or twice in a hundred years.[15] This situation often owed more to the poverty of the times than to a diminished sense of piety. In some parishes, there were scant financial resources for purchasing communion plate, tablecloths, tokens and even the elements. Moreover, well into the 18th century most impoverished country churches lacked seats, watertight roofs or wooden floors, appearing more analogous to "sheds for cattle than temples to God."[16] For many years after the Reformation, the pulpit and stool of penitence were among the few permanent indoor fixtures in Scottish churches. More affluent parishioners tended to bring their own stools to serve as seats placed in locations approved by the Kirk Session.[17] Squabbles invariably ensued over contested spaces and the beadle's staff, usually a long pole with a sharp point, proved an effective deterrent against disorderly behaviour. On Communion Sunday, the beadle's interventions helped preserve decorum and gravity, as he patrolled the church "to wauken sleepers, to drive out the dogs, and remove greetin bairns."[18] However, in 1597, the beadle apparently was no match for the overly zealous participants at a communion in Stirling when they rushed the table shouting and "spilling wine."[19] At this time, the virtually bare church interiors provided a convenient venue for communion. Tables, consisting of wooden planks on supports, were covered with linen cloths and surrounded by a paling-like enclosure that limited access to communicants who gained entry via two entrances. Here were stationed elders who monitored the collection of tokens and the admission of the worthy recipients of communion.

Throughout the 17th century, church officials implemented policies aimed primarily at regularizing sacramental practices and enforcing obedience to the laws of the Church. Still, irregularities and local variations prevailed. There was little uniformity even in such basic details as the choice of elements. Some communities used shortbread while others opted for white bread. In northeast Scotland, diced bread was the custom, whereas parishioners in Orkney favoured a type of oatcake. Claret or port seemed to be the most popular forms of communion wine. By the 1640s, the custom of outside services became increasingly commonplace as attendance at sacramental gatherings swelled. The favourite location was the churchyard adjacent to the church where participants sat on gravestones, benches or rough lawn. The tradition served many practical functions, most notably cost savings, as neighbouring parishes were able to pool their resources to offset the expenses of communion observances. According to Thomas Burns, the custom of the large communion at a central location, which began as a "response to the exigencies of the time," became "rooted in the popular mind" and took hold of their "affections."[20] It gained particular favour among the Gaelic-speaking inhabitants of Argylshire, Inverness-shire, Ross-shire, Sutherlandshire, Caithness-shire and the Western Isles.

In the opinion of historian John MacInnes, these sacramental gatherings had a salutary side effect—namely the destruction of "the lingering elements of district and clan antipathies by bringing people together under conditions eminently conducive to friendliness."[21] It is doubtful that Church officials fully appreciated this positive benefit. For them, the event painfully highlighted the futility of regulation. They were powerless to suppress the propensity of communicants, pilgrims and spectators, as well as so-called "Vagrants and sturdy beggars," to travel in crowds to the Sacrament.[22]

The General Assembly grew increasingly frustrated by their inability to impose regular observance of the Sacrament in every parish and they bemoaned the rising spectre of public disorder. Some of the attendance figures for these events are staggering. At the famed Cambuslang sacrament on August 15, 1743, there were 30,000 people in attendance, of whom 3,000 were communicants.[23] At the Communion in Mauchline during the late 18th century, the beadle was heard bellowing to the preacher "to fire away, for the 17th table was filling, and there was no end to the work."[24]

Admittedly, these events also served as a market place for horse-trading and cattle bargaining, as well as magnets for all kinds of impious behaviour including sexual dalliances, alcohol consumption and jostling around nearby stalls selling bread, cheese and ale. According to Dr. James Russell's reminiscences:

> ...at the Sacraments in Ettrick and Yarrow, baps of bread and barrels of ale were planted around the churchyard enclosure for purchase and use. When a popular preacher mounted the rostrum, a rush was made to the tent, but when 'a waufhand' turned up, the baps and barrels carried the day.[25]

Robbie Burns's poetical satire "The Holy Fair," written in 1785, brought public scandal to the Church and gave considerable notoriety to Presbyterian Scotland's great religious festival and its inherent abuses. Burns witnessed first-hand the unseemly mix of saints and sinners at sacramental gatherings in his native Ayrshire and could not resist satirizing their false piety and hypocritical hijinks:

> Howe monie hearts this day converts
> O' sinners and o'lasses
> Their hearts o'stane, gin night, are gane
> As saft as ony flesh is.
> There's some are fou o'love divine,
> There's some are fou o'brandy;
> An' monie jobs that day begin,
> May end in houghmagandie
> Some ither day.[26]

In the late 18th century, as evangelical religion gained impetus, there were "widespread" changes in the devotional life of Scottish Presbyterians.[27] According to religious historians, Andrew L. Drummond and James Bulloch, there was an increase in the "emotional content of Scottish devotion, a subjectivism, and an awareness of the personal and inward consequences of belief."[28] A more reverential attitude toward the Lord's Supper became increasingly pervasive as Highland evangelical ministers viewed the Communion Season with "utmost seriousness" and regarded it as "serving exclusively religious ends." In short, it was a vehicle for spiritual revival and renewal.[29] The impact of the sacramental experience at the Kiltearn Communion in 1785 was profound:

> There was an extraordinary manifestation of the Saviour's
> gracious presence in the congregation ... when, the service
> concluded, many of the Lord's people, from their ecstasy
> of soul and joy of spirit did not know whether they were in
> the body or out of the body.[30]

Long distances were no impediment to zealous pilgrims. Parishioners flocked to hear the preacher-idols of the day—Lachlan MacKenzie of Lochcarron, Ross-shire, John McDonald of Ferintosh and John Kennedy of Kilearnan. Some of the clergy were especially stringent in their efforts to purify the tradition and restore its solemnity by attempting to sever the link between Christian fellowship and communal festivity.

Two anecdotes demonstrate the complexity of this religious festival that was both holy day and holiday. The first story relates to a famous communion in Eriboll during a drought-ridden summer around 1789. The heat was scorching; even the streams had run dry. The multitude who gathered for worship were "faint and parched." On the Saturday, however, to the people's amazement, "a stream of water" suddenly gushed from the stones of the sandy beach behind the tent where the minister had delivered his sermon. The occurrence was pronounced a miracle and it became a treasured memory of the pious who dubbed the occasion *"Tobar freagradh urhuigh,"* ("the spring answer to prayer").[31]

The second story relates to a practical joke played on the Rev. Neil McBryde of Eriboll around 1799-1800. After administering the communion at Eriboll, he headed for Kinlochbervie with his creel filled with bread and wine and the communion plate. Or so he thought. When he arrived at his destination, he discovered that someone had tampered with his load and replaced it with sod and stones. The local people railed against the "miscreants at Eriboll" and never forgave the slight, long grumbling about the communion when they had to make do with baked scones and wine served in stoneware.[32] It would seem, then, that the communion season embodied elements of the sacred and the profane, of reverence and revelry.

At the height of the Celtic diasporic movements in the late-18th and early-19th centuries, as various tributaries of Scottish immigrants flowed to Canada, the traditional open-air communion was replicated in various permutations in such strongholds of Scottish Presbyterianism as Nova Scotia, Prince Edward Island and eastern Ontario. This cultural transplant, however, proved most resilient in its new soil of Cape Breton where it survived into the early 20th century. Now draped in the heavy folds of memory, which obscure its shape and form, this once-revered tradition remains a powerful symbol of the sturdy faith of Cape Breton's early Presbyterian church and its people.

Chapter Two

The Days of Sweet Gospel

Among the Scottish immigrants who came to Cape Breton during the early 19th century, old habits died hard. Their first recorded communion was held in River Inhabitants in 1834, although communions were undoubtedly observed at an earlier date at Mabou which had a settled minister by the early 1820s.[1] With the increased influx of ministers during the mid-19th century, the Presbyterian population demonstrated a heightened attachment to the tradition. Contemporary clergy reported: "We are much gratified observing the increased interest with which our people regard the dispensation of this divine ordinance amongst them from time to time."[2] By the 1850s, these summer gatherings, held between June and October at central locations, attracted thousands of people, sometimes numbering as high as six thousand.[3] By any standard, the number of people who attended communions in Cape Breton was astounding. Even as late as September 1892, the communion at Mira drew some five to six thousand.[4]

For sacramental-season pilgrims who made a complete tour of these communions on the island, travelling rock-strewn winding roads, along windswept coasts and through rugged hills, these events of fellowship, worship and commemoration were "times of refreshing."[5] For clergy, the open-air sacraments afforded opportunities for collegial interaction, as they travelled to neighbouring regions to assist in preaching and administering of the sacrament. Still, these advantages were often achieved at the expense of great physical exhaustion as the Revs. Hugh McLeod, Matthew Wilson and Alexander Farquharson discovered during one communion season which found them "footsore and hungry," lost in some remote, mountainous stretch in Cape Breton.[6] The three clerical wanderers were greatly relieved when they stumbled upon a lonely hut with a large pot of fish and potatoes boiling over a fire. Hunger overtook decorum, and all three men sampled the pot's contents, while the lone female occupant, alarmed by the arrival of three strange men on her doorstep, took to the woods in fright.

Each year, Cape Breton Presbyterian communities anticipated the five-day communion with a mixture of elation and dread. Spiritual preparations commenced several weeks in advance of the tramping pilgrims and rattling wagons crowded with whole families. Family worship was more rigorously observed, and elders busied themselves visiting and catechizing church members. Residents were motivated to pay their bills and settle old disputes.[7] Customarily, one month before the Lord's Supper, communicants accused of misconduct were called before the Session to "answer charges."[8] The "honour of religion" required both an explanation and expression of remorse for alleged "errors" before readmission to the Lord's Table.[9] Clearly, this annual event was a compelling incentive to put one's spiritual and worldly affairs in order. But, more importantly, these preparations constituted a symbolic public cleansing and communal reconciliation.[10]

This tradition also required elaborate logistical arrangements, for "all homes would be open and prepared for all the people who attended these services."[11] According to one source, the preparations for Sacrament Week at Baddeck Forks began as early as Monday morning. For the "women folks," the onset of the Communion Season meant a marathon of house cleaning, not just their own houses but the Lord's. The church had to look "its best on the great week of the sacra-

Fig. 1 "Sacramental scene in a western forest" From Joseph Smith, Old Redstone; or Historical Sketches of Western Presbyterianism, its Early Ministers, its Preilous Times, and its First Records. *Philadelphia: Lippincott, Grambo & Co., 1854. Lith of P. S. Duval & Co., Phil.*

ment."[12] There were floors and benches to be scrubbed, walls to be whitewashed and communion bread to be baked. Much more onerous for the women, especially those living near the church grounds, was the cooking and baking. They prepared vast quantities of food for the visitors who had to be well fortified to endure the physical rigors of five days of lengthy sermons and services. Most households put aside a supply of herring and stockpiled oatcakes, biscuits, pies and loaves. "I remember," later recalled the Rev. Charles MacDonald, "one woman who made bread. She got a barrel of flour before the Sacrament started at North River. She made bread of the barrel of flour, and it was said, when the Sacrament was over, there was nothing left but a grain."[13] Catherine Ross's mother, at Bucklaw, worked almost two days straight baking molasses and sugar cookies, and bread. Dolly MacKay recalled that her mother cooked for almost a week, preparing bannock, bread, cookies and pies for the onslaught of guests who arrived for the Boularderie Communion from Leitches Creek, Loch Lomond and Baddeck.[14] In Framboise and Gabarus, the "sacramental season" was marked by the baking of molasses cookies, known locally as "communion biscuits."[15]

Judging from published and oral accounts, the consumption of food during the late-19th century communions in Cape Breton was substantial.[16] According to the Rev. Charles MacDonald, it was customary to slaughter a sheep or a lamb, to ensure that there was sufficient food on hand.[17] In 1994, Mrs. Jessie Morrison of Baddeck recalled that her mother, in preparation for the huge appetites of her communion season guests, filled a barrel in her pantry with loaf bread. Neither fish nor loaves escaped the brunt of this invasion. In Wreck Cove, Alexander Smith's grandfather's guests quickly made short order of his half barrel of salt herring.[18] In *Harper's New Monthly Magazine* (1886), Charles H. Farnham recalled that his host's table groaned under the weight of potatoes, salt fish, butter, bread, milk, bannocks and tea. During this period, the breakfast diet consisted of a hearty mixture of potatoes, dried cod or herring, along with buckwheat bannock, oatcakes and strong tea. The early evening tea featured white flour bread, sweet cakes, curds and cheese, which was followed by a supper of porridge and clabbered milk. After the Sabbath service, the meal frequently consisted of mutton and salt ham, accompanied by potatoes and turnips.[19] Whiskey was also an integral part of the foodways during the communion season; that is, before the incursions of the temperance movement with its hyperbolic rhetoric about the evils of alcohol.[20]

For women, the sacramental season was synonymous with hard work as their households were transformed into hives of activity. Reflecting on his early 20th-century childhood in Seal Cove, Cape Breton, Angus Hector MacLean recalled:

> On such days many people called at our home for lunch,
> and the yard would be full of buggies and horses....
> Mother cooked as fast as she could, and then she and
> the girls served one table after another. The dining table
> seated about ten people, and I can recall five tables being
> served....[21]

The physical strain took a toll on Will Pringle's mother at The Points, West Bay. In his reminiscences, *Pringle's Mountain*, he wrote: "she made many loaves of home made bread and seventeen pies and ... her feet got so sore that she had to put her knee on a chair."[22] However tempting it is to construe such labours as indicative of female servitude and subjugation, it is clear that the women took great pride in the ingenuity and skill required to produce sufficient supplies of food and drink to meet the demands of the communion season.

Not only did the host family have to feed a multitude of guests, but their horses as well, depleting both cupboards and hay mow. Although the women shouldered much of the burden of hospitality, family members were also pressed into service: daughters participated in the domestic scurry, while sons busied themselves tending to the visitors' horses. For children, the pressures of additional chores and eating "leftovers in the kitchen" were offset by the exciting novelty of the sacramental season.[23] Although raised in a manse in Caithness, Scotland, Alastair Phillip's sentiments undoubtedly paralleled the Cape Breton experience when he wrote: "The children ... never considered it a proper Communion if they were able to sleep in their own beds," for the often costly expressions of hospitality also extended to lodging.[24] After all, guests not only had to be fed, but housed.

Arriving without formal invitation, the guests encamped in local houses, often overflowing into the barns. But the situation was not as haphazard as it sounds. There was a clearly established etiquette for the makeshift sleeping arrangements based on age and gender. The elderly visitors and couples slept in beds, while the parlour floor was allocated to the young girls who improvised with *seids* or "field beds."[25] The young men were accommodated in the barn or carriage house and outfitted with blankets and quilts spread on straw. Where inadequate space did not permit the complete segregation of the sexes, males and females were consigned to opposite sides of the room; if this area was filled to capacity, propriety then dictated that the men and women at the middle of the room sleep head to head.[26] In some households, it was not uncommon to have a dozen visitors sleeping on the kitchen floor. Roman Catholic neighbours also helped relieve the pressures of this inundation of Presbyterian pilgrims. Dorothy MacDonald Pottie of Glendale, River Denys Mountain, recalls that her family's Catholic household always bulged with visitors during the Communion season; Cape Breton's sectarian fault line was blurred during the Sàcramaidas "their common Highland blood proved thicker than holy water."[27]

According to Will Pringle of Pringle's Mountain, the typical communion season household could run to twelve visiting guests. An early contemporary account suggests that forty and even more sometimes lodged in one house.[28] Farnham placed the figure as high as fifty to seventy-five.[29] The local manse was also besieged by extra company. It is reported that one Cape Breton manse during the summer communion season of 1897 entertained at least thirty people.[30]

Hospitality and family honour were key ingredients in these sacramental gatherings. No remuneration exchanged hands, and no one was turned away from the door.[31] In the event that the host's house had no available room, the unfortunate late guest was accorded a meal while alternate accommodation nearby was arranged—to do anything less was a serious breach of the ethics of hospitality.[32] One late 19th-century account relates how a farmer near Baddeck Forks went into debt "to the tune of a hundred dollars because of his good naturedness."[33] Journalists unfamiliar with the region and its traditions invariably condemned the material costs and burdens of these "religious raids," failing to appreciate the underlying dynamics of a society where food was an essential medium for socializing.[34] These same outsiders also did not understand that the ability to feed and house such multitudes, especially for those settlers who had endured extreme privation, must have conferred considerable prestige.[35] Such gestures of kindness were not completely altruistic, however, for there was an underlying assumption that their generosity would be reciprocated when the host's family travelled to other communions. For some, there was also the much-prized privilege of sheltering and feeding the visiting clergy and elders assisting at the communion. In Cape Breton households, visiting clergy always had prior claim on the spare bedroom. In this context, hospitality found its highest reward, for these godly men more than repaid their hosts with blessings and the bread of life.

The Fast Day

The Cape Breton Presbyterian communion season was a five-day event which unfolded at a distinctive pace. Each day had its own special name and featured a scripted performance of prayers, psalms and sermons, all expressly designed to foster a purity and piety of thought and action. Self-examination, repentance and renewed obedience prevailed throughout the communion season in strict Presbyterian households.[36] Local business was usually suspended during this period of religious observance. According to Catherine Ross, her father observed the sanctity of the sacramental season by shutting down his sawmill in Bucklaw on Thursday.[37] Catherine Poole of Whycocomagh, born in 1902, remembered that the road crews stopped working at this special time.[38] Each day, the numbers of participants increased, foregathering for the main event, the Sabbath open-air communion.

The first day of the sacramental season was called *Là Traisg* (The Day of Fasting), ostensibly a day of fasting and preparation. Only the most devout abstained from food until the afternoon and then partaking "only in slight refreshment."[39] At Strathlorne, in 1889, there was an English service at 11 o'clock, followed by a Gaelic service which lasted until 2 o'clock and another in English, scheduled for the evening.[40] The Fast Day never attracted the crush of worshippers who gathered for the Sabbath communion. In fact, the first day of the sacramental season was clearly losing status by the 1860s. For example, at the Fast Day at West Bay in July 1864, "the people were not out in so great numbers as might have been expected."[41] By the turn of the century, it was abandoned by some congregations as they moved from a five-day communion to a more abbreviated three-day format.[42]

The Day of Self-Examination

Là na Ceist (The Day of Questioning), often styled as "the Men's day," was regarded in Cape Breton as "the greatest day of the five except the Sabbath day."[43] During much of the 19th century, the attendance at this Friday service was usually "very large."[44] This day of testimonials was "generally held in the open air" and was looked forward to with anticipation, for it offered the one opportunity in the year to "open out, explain and have explained" the spiritual perplexities pondered throughout the year.[45] In this way, the second day of the sacramental season often proved to be instructive and heart-searching. It could also be a protracted affair, judging from the three and one-half hour Ceist in Cape North during the autumn of 1882.[46] Commenting on the Friday service's popularity, a visiting minister observed in 1864: "There can be no doubt that these services have a powerful influence on the mind and heart of the great mass of our Gaelic congregations at the Communion season."[47] Although preaching was traditionally provided in both languages during the communion season, "The Men's day" was "generally in Gaelic only."[48] For example, at Strathlorne, in 1889, the Ceist, which ran from 11 until 2 o'clock, was conducted almost entirely in Gaelic.[49]

At the Friday service, the minister conducted the opening devotional exercises. The balance of the Ceist, however, was given over to discussion of the "Question" proposed by one of Na Daoine (the people), noted "old Christian inquirers."[50] The "Question" was based on some passage of scripture that was read or quoted and then dissected by members of this special brotherhood of godly laymen. Their commentary invariably hinged on identifying the "marks" or "tokens" of genuine grace. In short, the line of demarcation between saints and sinners was charted. The minister led off this discussion and then invited, sometimes from a prepared list, those best qualified "to speak to the question." The traditional Ceist was completely unrehearsed and extempore, and "the Men" cited scriptural passages, even whole chapters with amazing accuracy from memory, and described their own experiences of spiritual grace. These orations could last "a greater part of the day" for there was no fixed number of participants.[51] At Grand River's Ceist in 1890, fourteen "spoke to the question."[52] That same year, twenty-two men participated in Mira's Friday service.[53] Often two questions were posed and discussed successively, before the minister offered his closing summation—confirming, expanding and correcting as he judged needful. When discussion drew to a close, the individual who proposed the initial Question offered a prayer. The Ceist day ended with psalm singing and a benediction by the minister.

The tradition of "the Men" was not indigenous to Cape Breton. It originated in Sutherland and Ross-shire, Scotland, where a body of pious and "anxious Inquirers" were revered for their fervent piety, personal experience of religion and second sight.[54] During the eighteenth century, "the Men" formed a venerable lay elite to whom was given the privilege of controlling the Friday Fellowship meetings to the virtual exclusion of the minister. Socially, however, "the Men" tended to be of humble origin and devoid of educational pretensions; occasionally, sheep farmers were found among their ranks, but never factors.[55] Although frequently illiterate, they possessed an unerring knowledge of Scripture and roved freely over the Highlands, functioning not only as catechists and mystics, but also as guardians of the Sabbath. Of Colin Sutherland of Helmsdale it was said, "Though quite unable to read, he was possessed of a powerful mind and retentive memory. If any person reading the bible missed or mispronounced a word, he would correct him."[56] One Highlander, familiar with the tradition of "the Men," wrote:

> It is quite impossible to avoid feeling the deepest pity for the poor clergy on a sacrament Friday ... so high was the superiority of "the Men" in native talent, and still higher the degree to which these talents were exercised by Divine truth.[57]

Readily identifiable because of their long hair, black cloaks and spotted handkerchiefs, "the Men" had a preponderant influence on the public mind. Their maxims became imbedded in folk memory and their descriptions of the genuine tokens of saving grace were widely accepted as the exemplar. During the 18th century, they gained notoriety as they watchdogged regular ministers, verbalized public discontent and introduced an element of accountability between the ministers and parishioners. In many ways, "the Men" were a more effective intermediary between God and the Highlanders than the ministers, whose credibility was sometimes undermined by their uncomfortably-close alliance with the landlords. In some instances, "the Men" even set up rival services.[58] As early as 1737, the Synod of Ross and Caithness, which viewed "the Men" as a threat to the established church, attempted to curtail their activities and suppress the Friday Fellowship meetings.[59] Nevertheless, the General Assembly revoked the Synod's act twenty years later. Thus freed from legal constraints, "the Men" continued to thrive, generating both spiritual vitality as well as religious dissension and helping pave the way for the Free Church doctrine in many Highland parishes.[60]

"The Men" emerged as a significant force in the Pres-byterian Church in Nova Scotia. The traditional members of the Church of Scotland continued to view them with suspicion in their new environment. So, too, did a Church of Scotland deputation that visited Pictou in 1856; to them, this sort of lay instruction fostered "spiritual pride."[61] In Cape Breton, however, "the Men" flourished and retained many of their original powers. In fact, owing to the initial dearth of ministers, they oftentimes functioned as lay catechists and lay preachers. They conducted prayers, visited the sick and held periodic meetings in people's houses where the catechism was recited and its teachings explained. Even after the formal establishment of the Cape Breton Presbytery, these religious luminaries continued to command a respect bordering on veneration. Few were educated, and many of them could not read. Still, they were celebrated for their godliness, their oratorical gifts and their deep personal familiarity with the workings of grace. One writer who had observed them first hand remarked: "The illustrations used were sometimes from familiar scenes of farm life, and sometimes from the great writers and preachers of the olden days, Bunyan being oftenest quoted."[62] Their influence, it seems, extended to both young and old. One elderly man reminisced: "I never saw a man I loved as I loved Duncan [Ban]. I was then wild and careless, but I was never happier than when listening to his presentation of the story of the cross."[63]

During the sacramental season, "the Men" often walked eighty to one hundred miles, from one communion to the next, presiding over the Ceist and conducting prayer meetings.[64] For example, at the summer communion at Leitches Creek in 1889, "the Men" in attendance represented a cross-section of Cape Breton communities, including Cow Bay, Boularderie, Sydney, The Forks, Coxheath and Mira.[65]

For the Rev. Malcolm MacPhail, one-time minister at the Scotch Presbyterian Church in Boston, Cape Breton's Friday service was an impressive spectacle of "strong witticisms" and "keen observations" as well as biblical erudition. It also served as the context of his vivid recollection of an exchange between an elderly woman and a boy, the former preoccupied with pious thoughts, the latter engaged in childish pranks directed against a big toad which had strayed into the midst of the open-air meeting. When the child delivered a kick that sent the toad "sprawling," the old woman registered her disapproval with a scowl and reproached him in a "loud whisper" in Gaelic. From her perspective, it was the child, not the toad, who was an unwelcome intruder at the solemn occasion.[66]

According to contemporary accounts, the Friday audiences were seldom impassive. At one late 19th-century Cape Breton Ceist, some of the male spectators responded to the discourses of various "Men" with loud exclamations of assent and satisfaction. Conversely, the women did not give vent to their emotions in such an audible, verbal way. They sat, their bodies swaying rhythmically backwards and forwards as they clutched handkerchiefs. Their cheeks streamed with tears, but their "voices were not heard."[67] Their behaviour, undoubtedly, was determined by the force of tradition that deemed the Ceist the "Men's day." In short, women were "not allowed to speak" at the male-dominated Ceist.[68] Margaret McPhail's novel, *Loch Bras D'Or*, depicts the fate of a much-troubled woman who, challenging this taboo, rose nervously to her feet to exclaim: "I have no one to speak for me." "Woman sit down!... You have but to listen and derive solace and knowledge from the speakers, men who are moved by the holy spirit" was the thundering rebuke.[69] The audience, men and women alike, stared disapprovingly at her as if "a dog had come into the church and barked."[70] They regarded the young woman's actions as a violation of the gendered code of the

Ceist. Even as late as the 1930s, this practice prevailed. Some older North Shore residents still remember when Agnes MacRitchie piped up in English with her own response to the question. The audience was stunned by her brazen outburst, though did not judge her too unkindly. She was known to be a "very capable" woman, and her indiscretion was pardoned because of her inexperience. After all, she was "only here as a visitor"; although later informants could not recall with any certainty if she came from the United States or belonged to Boularderie.[71]

Inherent in the 19th-century sacramental season was a patriarchal bias and a clear division of labour and prescribed etiquette; women did not participate fully or creatively as equals. One cleric aptly summed up the situation when he reported that the women assisted in their "own sphere" with their "Mary-like conversation" and their "Martha-like hospitality."[72]

How does one account for this gendered discrepancy in audience behaviour? Were these women constrained by the Victorian dictates of feminine modesty and decorum? Were they repressed by the wide-spread conviction that women speaking in church was unscriptural? One explanation for the derivation of the term "the Men" asserts that this terminology did not relate to gender, but served only to differentiate between this special class of laity and the clergy. This argument, however plausible, fails to explain why the Ceist was monopolized by men. One suspects that few women were audacious enough to challenge the ban on their active involvement at the Friday service.[73] After all, even in such matters as family worship, their voices were muted as those of the male members of the household prevailed; the women only said grace in the men's absence.[74]

Although quietly patient during the Ceist, the women were not shy about expressing their views after the services and during the mealtimes. As they bustled around the table, waiting on family and guests, women could monitor conversations, intervening at timely moments, exerting a proper authority of their own without straying far from their acknowledged womanly sphere. According to Catherine Ross, her grandmother often presided over post-Ceist discussions as the family gathered to eat in the cool shade of the house later in the afternoon. Her religious knowledge, usually framed in terms of a personal familiarity with God's ways, never failed to impress: "My Grandmother was talking as if she knew Him."[75]

The much-venerated brotherhood of "the Men" enjoyed a status "superior to that accorded the minister" and they were regarded by traditional clergy as professional rivals.[76] For this reason, there was some jealousy between the two groups. There was also mutual respect. One cleric, who heard "The flower of the 'men' of Cape Breton" at a Ceist in Middle River, conceded that any minister, whose "self-complacency be not altogether shell-proof" would after exposure to these laymen find his "grace and humility a little stirred up and increased."[77] Dr. Robert Burns was also moved to words of praise, impressed during his visit to Cape Breton in 1858 by the "number of intelligent 'men'" who had helped transform Boularderie into a stronghold of "evangelical truth and experimental religion."[78] After visiting Cape North in 1894, the Rev. M. A. McKenzie confessed that he was "struck" not only by the "stalwart" appearance of "the Men," but also by "their remarks, and style of expression."[79]

Certainly, there were clerics who were reluctant to trespass on the Friday proceedings. The Rev. Murdoch Stewart was visibly cowed by their prominence at the Ceist and wrote in his diary: "It was the first time I spoke at any of these meetings—Much against my will I was forced to speak but it was very little—only telling one anecdote."[80] Later clergy also acquiesced to the protocol of the Ceist. An account of a Ceist at Mira in June 1904 reads: "There wasn't a lot for the ministers to do; we can't put 'wind in the feathers'."[81] Professional jealousies aside, few clergy could begrudge "the Men" admiration. There is no more eloquent tribute to this spiritual fraternity than that penned by the Rev. Donald MacOdrum, one-time minister at Mira:

> They were respected, reverenced, loved. Their power
> was not of office but of character. Their words were with
> authority, because they came from the heart throbbing

> with life. When they spoke of the sacred majesty of God's
> law men perceived that the words had meaning....[82]

The antagonisms which erupted in some Highland parishes between these eminent laymen and ordained clergy seem to have had no parallel in Cape Breton. The early Presbyterian clergy in Cape Breton, such as the Rev. James Fraser and Dr. Hugh McLeod, openly acknowledged the special gifts of these laymen. They harnessed their pastoral talents and recruited their assistance, usually as elders and precentors, viewing them as a vital adjunct in those regions deprived of settled ministers. In fact, in most instances, "the Men," rather than operating as free agents beyond its purview, were incorporated into mainstream Presbyterian polity.

Among these pious laymen were several individuals who became celebrities at Cape Breton's 19th-century Ceists.[83] For example, Boularderie's Duncan MacDonald (Donnchadh Bàn Ceistear—"fair-haired Donald the catechist") was one of Cape Breton's most celebrated "Men." A native of Coll, Hebrides, this lay catechist-farmer was widely respected for his charismatic evangelical discourses. During prayer meetings, his homilies were often so intense that distraught participants had to be removed to another room so that the meeting could be continued. According to his obituary, his impact on the Ceist was equally profound:

> On the Friday of our communion throughout the Island
> Duncan was anxiously looked for; and if absent, which
> was seldom the case, there was a blank which was felt,
> not only by the people, but also by the brethren. Of all the
> Catechists and Men Duncan Macdonald was acknowl-
> edged to be the first.[84]

MacDonald's discourses were far above the commonplace. In fact, some of his allegories and adages were quickly incorporated into Cape Breton's store of religious knowledge along with Scripture and psalms, the most memorable of which was his remonstrance against gossipers: "It is not for the purpose of goring the lambs that horns were put on sheep."[85] His words were still being quoted sixty years after his death, an event that inspired Effie MacLeod of North River to write a fulsome elegy in 1854 that ran to no less than thirty-five verses.[86]

Another important member of this spiritual band was the farmer-catechist-precentor, Donald Ross of Cow Bay (now Port Morien). A native of Uig, Lewis, Ross worked as a catechist among the Presbyterians of Cow Bay, Mira and Catalone and frequently undertook "preaching tours" all over the island.[87] Widely acknowledged as a "man of God," arresting in appearance, and brimming with scripture and reborn zeal, Ross drew crowds. Few of "the Men" were as incisive or illuminating as he. He was regarded as one of the "ablest and most acceptable 'Ceist' day speakers," and according to the Rev. John Murray was "probably the best known, most highly gifted and greatly esteemed of them all [catechists]."[88]

Another popular figure on the communion-season circuit was Angus McLeod of Middle River. Nicknamed Aonghas Liath ("grey-haired Angus") because of his prematurely silvered hair, McLeod had all the hallmarks of the consummate "Man." He was pious, revered, commanding, strictly Calvinist and endowed with a resonant voice. His obituary declared: "He was very powerful in addressing a congregation in the Gaelic language of which he had great command, with seldom or never a word out of joint...."[89] Donald McDonald, a Gaelic precentor from Mira, who was reborn at an advanced age, was rated one "of the very sweetest of the 'Men'."[90] His "childlike faith," his "power in prayer" and "marvelous" acquaintance with scripture and his "winsome" pleading voice mesmerized audiences who gathered for the Friday services.[91] Mira's Donald McDougall also captivated listeners at the Ceist "for seldom did he pray in public without melting many to tears."[92]

Hugh Ferguson, an elder from Gabarus Lake, affectionately known as "Little Hugh of Gabarus," was also widely acknowledged as "peculiarly gifted of God."[93] Those who heard him speak often remarked on his "sweet melancholy voice," which when overcome with "fervor and ecstasy," often broke into a strange, involuntary yelp.[94] This eccentricity apparently did not repel listeners. Nor did Baddeck's Donald Murdoch MacAulay's unusual eye defect. Despite a half-closed eye, Dòmhnall Mhurchaidh Bhàin ("Donald, son of fair-haired Murdoch") charmed the audiences gathered at his feet, with the musicality of his voice, eloquence of expression and genial disposition. He was not as morose as some of his contemporaries and had few equals. In fact, "at the summer communions throughout the island no speaker was in greater demand."[95]

At North River, St. Ann's, Donald MacDonald (Dòmhnall Ceistear—"Donald the Catechist"), who divided his time between preaching, teaching and farming, was celebrated for his "instinctive insight into divine truth." For weeks prior to the sacrament, he visited homes in the far-flung congregation, conducting prayer meetings and tutoring adherents in the Shorter Catechism and the Confession of Faith.[96] In West Bay, the Harris-born John Shaw was a storehouse of sacred truths, which "sanctified his character to a high degree." According to the *Presbyterian Witness*, the words delivered by this elder at the open-air communions "were an inspiration to the preachers."[97] Whycocomagh also boasted members of this spiritual aristocracy including Archibald MacKinnon, a farmer and carpenter, who "could preach a wonderful sermon in the Gaelic language," and the catechist, John MacKenzie, who was a frequent speaker at the Ceist and passed on a legacy of Gaelic tunes to Cape Breton's early precentors.[98]

Another leading participant during the sacramental season was Angus McLean from Cape North. He stood out from his contemporaries with his long dark bushy hair, his gaunt sallow face, and his raspy voice. His whole being stirred with an inner intensity and he projected the appearance of "an ascetic."[99] In the isolated and scattered settlements of Cape North, he laboured to maintain a Presbyterian presence during the long absences of settled clergy. Here again was a person of impressive oratorical prowess. The Rev. A. Farquharson pronounced him "a man of extraordinary talents.... Seldom have I heard his equal in prayer."[100] The Rev. Malcolm Campbell also wrote about the Cape North lay preacher in superlatives, claiming that McLean's "gift of prayer was his in fuller measure than that of any man the writer has ever listened to either in pulpit or pew."[101]

In Big Bras d'Or, Donald Mac-Dermid, born in Wreck Cove, Victoria County, in 1845, belonged to this special caste of laymen. In his early career, MacDermid found employment with lumber gangs in Maine and CPR construction crews in Western Canada, but it was as an elder at St. James Presbyterian Church in Big Bras d'Or that MacDermid came to public prominence. He was revered for his familiarity with the Gaelic bible and his oratorical talents when propounding "The Question." One admirer remarked, "On Ceist Day everybody waited with great expectation for Donald MacDermid to get up."[102] Middle River Presbyterian elder, Kenneth MacLennan, also had an honoured position at local Ceists. His credentials as a Ceist-day participant were impeccable. Not only was he father of two Cape Breton divines—Rev. Neil MacLennan and Rev. Dr. A. K. MacLennan, both stationed in Boston—and grandfather of Rev. Dr. David MacLennan, one-time minister at the Timothy Eaton Memorial United Church in Toronto, but he also possessed many of the requisite endowments guaranteed to draw and impress Ceist-day audiences, namely a fluency in Gaelic and a powerful spiritual engagement. Shortly after MacLennan's death in 1913, one admirer noted:

Fig. 2 Donald MacDermid (b.1845), "a prominent Cape Dauphin Gael." The Canadian-American Gael, *Vol. 1. 1931: 88.*

> It was a rare treat to listen to him (always in Gaelic of course) either lecturing on a passage of Scripture when conducting a prayer meeting or speaking at the fellowship meeting

Fig. 3 Kenneth MacLennan (1826-1913), "an outstanding Middle River Gael." The Canadian-American Gael, *Vol. 1. 1931: 88.*

39

> on the "Ceist Day"—the men's day of the Communion season. Moreover he was a power in the prayer meeting or cottage gathering and he possessed unusual eloquence and fervency in pouring forth his soul in prayer to God to whom he seemed to have access with peculiar nearness.[103]

James M. MacLeod of North River, Victoria County, achieved the status of a household name as one of "Cape Breton's worthies." This one-time manager of MacKay MacAskill's store at North River Bridge outshone many of his Ceist-day peers. His noble countenance, strong faith and keen Christian insight all bore the stamp of a saintly man. It was at the summer season open-air services that MacLeod gained notoriety. He was, according to the Rev. J. A. MacLellan, "THE MAN WAITED FOR BY ALL."[104] The respect he commanded was abundantly displayed when he died in March 1910. No fewer than 450 people, drawn from a radius of forty miles, attended his funeral at the North River Church.[105]

By the 1930s and 1940s, the numbers in this exclusive group of spiritual leaders were dwindling. Among those wearing the mantle in the 1940s was Kenneth "Kennie" MacLeod of North River Bridge, St. Ann's, who enjoyed at this time the distinction of being Cape Breton's only Gaelic colporteur. A

silver-tongued Gaelic speaker, he was a popular guest at Victoria County's religious and secular gatherings, and his turn on Ceist day was "awaited with great expectancy."[106]

One of the last of the Ceist-day notables was Malcolm MacDonald of Tarbot, Victoria County, who died in November 1945. With his melodious voice and deep sense of Christian calling, he stood at the forefront of the Ceist-day participants, a remnant of the "old school of 'men of the church'."[107] This one-time schoolmaster, farmer and general store owner spent a lifetime immersed in God's words and works as a Sunday School

Fig. 4 Councillor Kenneth MacLeod, North River, NS, c.1940s, "an eminent Gael." The Canadian American Gael, Vol. 2. 1948 (May): 15.

teacher, elder and clerk of session. No less than eight days before his death, he precented the Gaelic psalms as he had for fifty years. Inspired by the passing of this religious beacon, Malcolm MacAskill of North River penned the following words as a tribute:

> When he opened the Bible and read the truth
> How well he could tell the teachings of Glory.
> Friday at the Sacrament when they raised him up
> He spoke loudly and with joy about the Grace that gave
> him life.[108]

Despite their own individual idiosyncracies, Cape Breton's "Men" shared many striking similarities. They had reputations for godliness, as praying and labouring men whose lives, speech and actions were of a piece, each mirroring the fullness and piety of the other. Not only were they men of rich, interior spirituality and principle, but they were also gifted with oratorical powers, often leaning toward an allegorical, cryptic form of verbal expression—"a peculiar way of conceiving and expressing religious truths" was the way the Rev. John Murray phrased it.[109] Most importantly, they were all blessed with a deep personal familiarity with the workings of

Fig. 5 Malcolm MacDonald, Tarbot, NS. (1864-1945), "an eminent on Ceist day." The Canadian American Gael, Vol. 2. 1948 (May): 15.

grace. For example, Angus McLeod of Middle River and Donald Ross of Port Morien, both natives of Uig, Scotland, traced their conversions to the evangelical ministry of the celebrated Rev. Alexander McLeod of Lewis. This first-hand knowledge, it was popularly believed, endowed "the Men" with special spiritual insights and gave the words drawn from the depths of their own experience both authority and power. There was nothing counterfeit about their spiritual pretensions. As the Rev. D. MacOdrum declared, "when they opened their lips, young and old recognized that these men had been 'in the secret place of the Most High'."[110]

The Day of Preparation

Saturday was the "preparation day" devoted to two services, one in Gaelic and one in English. A richly descriptive account furnished by the Rev. James Fraser brings this event to life:

Fig. 6 North Shore, NS, St. Ann's Presbyterian Church precentors, c.1930s. (L to r, with "favourite tune" in brackets): Councillor Tommie MacDonald (Bangor), Neil R. MacDonald (St. Paul's), Malcolm Angus MacLeod (New London) and John Alex [John X.] MacDonald (St. David). The Canadian-American Gael, Vol. 1. 1931: 89.

Fig. 7 North Shore, St. Ann's, NS, United Church precentors, c.1930s. (L to r): Alex J. Morrison, Sandy K. Morrison, Philip MacLeod and K. A. Morrison, all of Wreck Cove, NS. The Canadian-American Gael, Vol. 1. 1931: 89.

Fig. 8 Precentors at St. Andrew's Church, North River, St. Ann's, NS, c.1930s. (L to r, with "favourite tune" in brackets): Malcom MacDonald, Tarbot (New London), Dan A. [Dannie Jim] MacLeod (St. David) and Chas. MacDonald (Colsell). The Canadian-American Gael, Vol. 1. 1931: 89.

> Were you to stand on a little eminence, during one of
> these mornings, you would see boats loaded with people
> coming from all directions, and making for a certain point,
> or small promontory; advance towards the place, and
> you see rather a handsome church, neatly painted white,
> a capacious schoolhouse building at one end at a little
> distance; at the other, and also at a little distance, a neat
> tent-box, and a venerable-looking man standing in front
> of it, holding an octavo Bible, and reading to the people as
> they assemble, and crowds of decent serious-like people,
> repairing to the spot, and quietly taking their seats on the
> grass; and at the point close, upwards of 100 boats newly
> drawn up. I should not forget ten years and upwards, very
> attentive—having their Bibles, and serious turning up, and
> marking any passages mentioned.[111]

Normally in the afternoon or evening, candidates for their first communion presented themselves to the Session for examination.[112] They would be interrogated about their knowledge of doctrine, performance of religious duties and experience of saving grace. On this occasion, much weight was placed on "correct views" and the personal recommendations of an elder.[113] Withholding sacramental privileges was not an arbitrary act. Adultery, lying, drunkenness, frolicking, poor attendance and unresolved personal disputes were grounds for the rejection or abrogation of a communicant's privileges. The commission, or even being suspected, of such acts was deemed an affront to both God and community. Dancing, for example, could dash one's chances of sitting at the Lord's Table. In St. George's Channel, drunkenness usually resulted in a two-year suspension from the church.[114] The fate of Mrs. Morrison, a resident of the same locale, was especially bleak. Her name was peremptorily struck from the communion rolls "because of misconduct while her husband was away."[115] After intensive cross-examination, the father of the illegitimate child was also disbarred from communion as "it was a heinous sin and brought reproach to the cause of Christ."[116] Still, despite popular stereotypes about the sturdy moralism of elders and the severity of local Sessions, a sampling of 19th-century Kirk Sessions records in Cape Breton indicates that the normal course was one of forbearance towards lapsed communicants.

Even in cases of moral turpitude, a public statement before the Session expressing repentance for trangressions and assurances to "live a life becoming the Gospel" was sufficient for reinstatement.[117]

The names of those authorized to receive the Sàcramaid were inscribed in the congregation's communion roll. Sometimes these entries were accompanied by editorial annotations, such as "God-fearing," "a loving, earnest Christian," "promising young woman," "a very pious woman" and "eminently a man of prayer."[118] It was common practice in some congregations for first-time communicants sanctioned by the Session to appear publicly before the congregation. Following an address to intending participants, communion tokens for admission to the Sàcramaid were handed out; the new communicants were given precedence in the ceremonial distribution of these vouchers of church membership.[119] The small coin-like tokens, often impressed with the scriptural text "This do in Remembrance of Me," as well as an image of a communion table, were the outward symbols signifying full fellowship with the Church and one's eligibility to sit at the "table" on the morrow.[120] Many Nova Scotian Presbyterian congregations used stock tokens, generic in their shape and design; others, however, were more individualized, bearing the name of the congregation and the name or initials of the minister. Interestingly enough, there is no evidence that the Gaelic language ever graced Cape Breton's communion tokens, although this convention prevailed in some Scottish Highland congregations. In the early years of pioneering settlement, the availability of tokens was problematic. Some ministers actually arrived from Scotland with a ready-made supply; some even brought the moulds or dies to produce them.

Fig. 9 A quantity of tokens from 1843. On one side: "Free Church of Scotland." On the other side: "Let a Man Examine Himself. I. Cor. XI.28."

Commemorative tokens from 1975 centenary. On one side: "Centennial 1975, The Presbyterian Church in Canada." On the other side: "This do in Remembrance of Me. I.Cor. XI.24."

In Scotland, tokens were sometimes carried by local residents moving to a new parish. This multi-purpose emblem of Christian character and good standing in one's home church not only opened the gate of heaven, but also helped pave the way for social acceptance.

Before nightfall, the communion table(s) and benches were set out in readiness for the Sabbath. Few ventured to the Lord's Table without following the prescribed protocol outlined above. One wonders what emboldened Miss McKinnon of East Lake Ainslie to communicate on July 29, 1912, without the Session's sanction. Fortunately for her, the Session chose a more discreet disciplinary course of action. Deeming her a "young woman of good Christian life and character," they agreed to admonish her for this irregularity "in private."[121]

Saturday was also preoccupied with more temporal concerns. Owing to the proscriptions against labour on the Sabbath, people shouldered a "double load" of chores on Saturday.[122] Most of the food for Sunday was prepared in advance. Of course, this was normal practice throughout the year, but during the Communion season, the volume of work was magnified. The observance of the sabbatarian rule was deeply imprinted on most people's consciences.[123] Any disregard of Sunday sanctity carried a heavy penalty, in both religious and social terms.[124] However, one suspects that the transgressor often feared public censure more than the wrath of God. An anecdote related by a resident of St. George's Channel implies as much:

> A woman went out to the field before sun-up on a Sunday to dig potatoes, a task which should have been performed on Saturday. On her return, her husband chastised her for working because the Lord would see her and punish her wrong-doing. She replied that the Lord would understand knowing that she had a large family to feed. He would consider all the circumstances involved. But, she was very concerned should a neighbour spot her—then she would really be condemned.[125]

In Cape Breton Presbyterian households all labour was to cease on Saturday at sundown; no exceptions were made even for harvest season. Hattie Carmichael of Meadow Road recalled: "We weren't supposed to pick an apple. If you were starving for an apple, you weren't supposed to take an apple off a tree. And you'd believe that. We thought about it every minute."[126] Kenny Angus Morrison of Framboise remembered his Sundays being bounded by stifling constraints: "On Sunday, if they caught you picking a berry, you'd be in for it. Not a stick of wood was brought in. You could clear the manure from under the cow, but you couldn't throw it out the window."[127] During the winter months, shifting the frozen manure on the following Monday presented all sorts of challenges. For children, Saturday night and Sunday must have seemed like a humourless, grey interlude in the week with its sanctions against chewing gum, playing cards and musical instruments—even curling one's hair.[128] In some families, Sabbatarianism was so strictly enforced that the receptacles for collecting maple sap were overturned on Saturday evening "so as not to gather Sunday dropping."[129] Nets and trawls were usually retrieved from the water that Saturday afternoon.

For the women, Saturday was "a big baking day, to go over Sunday."[130] Vegetables were washed and pared, the carcass of mutton was readied: "We were all ready there to put in the pots and on the stove."[131] Boots were cleaned, some faces shaved, firewood split and piled, gardens weeded, stoves polished and blacked, floors scrubbed with fine sand and water hauled in. Although the Sabbath rule permitted tending to the livestock and milking cows—deemed "works of necessity and mercy"—feed was removed from the mows and bins and set out for the following day "so as to require the least possible labor in feeding the animals."[132] For the fishermen at Grand River, it was considered a huge concession when the local Session in July 1884 gave them permission to leave their nets in the sea on Sunday, a deviation that was rationalized as "passive Sabbath fishing."[133]

The Day of Communion

The Sabbath was the climax of the five-day festival. The first four days were preparatory, all part of a crescendo of religious activities, culminating in the Sunday sacrament. This event drew the largest crowd during the season. The long trek was not for the faint of heart, some of the participants coming long distances. The Whycocomagh communions, for example, drew people from as far as Mabou, Baddeck, Margaree, Gut of Canso and even St. Ann's, while the Mira gatherings included visitors from Port Morien, Grand River, Framboise, Sydney and Boularderie.[134] Worshippers at the Boularderie communions in the 1850s hailed from Baddeck, West Bay, Malagawatch and Whycocomagh, distances varying from ten to forty miles. Sacrament Week at Baddeck Forks during the late 19th century attracted vast hordes from Whycocomagh, Englishtown and even as far as Cape North, almost a hundred miles away. Faithful pilgrims like Mrs. Alexander McKay and her neighbour, Mrs. Morrison, were undeterred by such physical obstacles as distance. They walked twenty-two miles to Middle River's communion from the Rear at Baddeck Bay, departing in the early morning "after milking the cows" and returning in time to complete their evening milking chores.[135] Mrs. Ken McDonald of Table, Boularderie, who lived to 103 years, was also a remarkable example of dogged devotion. In her advanced years, she used to walk to church, a distance of six miles, hobbling along with "the help of her staff."[136] Fortunately, during the summer communion season, these pilgrims benefited from the long daylight hours. Perhaps, they even stopped en route to break their journey at one of Cape Breton's fabled "rest stones"; these were recognized stopping places where people could rest and share food and religious conversation.[137] Elder William Kemp of Boularderie had his own righteous reasons for travelling on foot and preferred walking seven miles each way to the communion site rather than "having the trouble and care of a horse on the Lord's Day."[138]

As early as 9 o'clock, worshippers started assembling, and for almost two hours, "as far as our eyes could see," this steady swollen stream continued.[139] Few came supplied with food to stave off hunger throughout the long day, certainly no more than one or two morsels of oaten biscuit, or perhaps some wheaten biscuit, stashed in their pockets. More than likely, some had stopped at a nearby pump to drink some refreshing water. They came in all ages, but the most purposeful in their gait were the elderly pilgrims with their walking staffs who had "been to many a sacrament."[140] They cherished this day like the old "burly Scot" who came annually on his "pie-bald steed" to the Baddeck Forks Sàcramaid or Jessie McLean of Grand Bay, for whom an "old Gaelic bible worn to tatters" by daily use and the "open-air deliverances" were her main source of spiritual uplift.[141] Or like Neil McIntosh, an elder from Framboise, who despite a four-mile walk and his advanced age of 102, refused to miss this event during the 1880s. According to the *Presbyterian Witness*, he "gave personal attendance to everything connected with the tent, tables, collection boxes," revelling in "attending to everything appertaining to the Lord's ordinance."[142]

Fig. 10 Rev. Hugh McLeod (1803-1894), founder of Presbyterian Church at Mira Ferry, NS. Photo by: unknown, c.1848. Beaton Institute. 77-890-1024

Many people came to the communion sites on foot. In fact, barefoot travellers, even during the late-19th century, were not an uncommon sight. Hoping to spare their shoes, they frequently traversed the meadows barefoot, carrying their shoes and stockings in their hands or fastened to a rope around their waists.[143] These articles of clothing were donned when they reached the roadway; if the opportunity presented itself, they stopped to wash their feet in a nearby brook. The practice of carrying one's shoes and stockings to a Sabbath service was as much a mark of devoutness as poverty and economy. Footwear, especially among the early settlers who often wore larrigans (moccasins), was scarce and hence highly valued.[144] American historian Leigh Schmidt contends that "the simple act of clothing" one's feet as one approached a place of worship, especially for rural inhabitants who routinely went barefoot during the summer months, was an act of reverence.[145]

Pilgrimage to the communion season sites was not limited to foot travel. Others arrived on horseback, open buggies or carts, all heading towards a common centre. Sometimes, two women rode on a horse, but in many more cases the man occupied the saddle, while the woman sat behind him. At one of Baddeck Fork's late-19th-century sacraments, a witness counted as many as one hundred teams of horses on the west side of the field near the communion site. Only during the Communion Season was the ban against Sabbath travel by horse and carriage temporarily suspended. Invariably, the people travelled in clusters, for the very act of pilgrimage was "a corporate endeavour, an opportunity for fellowship, conviviality and shared devotion."[146]

In the early part of the 19th century, overland communication was extremely arduous and wheeled conveyances were rare. For example, when the Rev. Dr. Hugh McLeod first settled in Mira in 1850, there was only one wagon connected with the whole congregation. It belonged to a "gentleman" and was "pretty bulky," better suited "for state occasions."[147] Nevertheless, people were not easily discouraged in matters of faith, and all available means of transportation were pressed into service. During Mira's sacramental season in 1856, for instance, it was reported that "All vehicles in and around Sydney were in requisition on the occasion."[148] Later in the century, wheeled transport was more commonplace. The "carriages" which converged at St. Ann's summer-time communion in 1889 were reputedly "without number."[149] During the dry summers, the billowing clouds of dust, stirred up by the wheels of the carts and carriages, heralded the arrival of the sacramental season travellers.

Oftentimes, if the communion was situated near a body of water, the pilgrims also came by boat. In August 1852, at Mira's first communion season, the Mira River was studded with flats and boats of all dimensions bearing "thousands of Worshippers."[150] A fleet of twenty-one boats "full of people" was observed at St. Ann's open-air communion in 1889.[151] At least two crowded schooners conveyed people from the opposite shore of the harbour. Those visitors headed to the Whycocomagh, Boularderie and Little Narrows communions could always avail themselves of steamship connections on the Lakes. In September 1852, worshippers from the Mines and Sydney took passage on the steamer, *Banshee*, in order to attend the sacrament at Boularderie.[152] More than forty years later, this custom persisted. For example, in August 1894, two steamships from Baddeck, including the *May Queen*, conveyed a "large crowd" to the Lord's Supper at Little Narrows.[153] In the late 19th century, Catherine Ross's father at Bucklaw usually transported at least ten people to the Little Narrows communion in his sailboat. Many of his passengers were from Hume's Rear and did not possess a horse and wagon. On those days, her father prayed for "a good wind," but he was seldom deterred by rough weather, even if it was "blowing a gale of a wind."[154]

Even if one makes allowances for exaggerated attendance figures, the turnout at Cape Breton's 19th-century communions was impressive. The Boularderie and Whycocomagh communions of 1842 attracted upwards of 4,000 people "from all parts of the island."[155] At Mira's first communion in 1852, an estimated 4–5,000 worshippers congregated.[156] The same year, Boularderie's Lord's Supper attracted no fewer than 3–4,000.[157] In July 1853, at least 8,000 people gathered at Whycocomagh.[158] According to oral tradition, there were 200 boats anchored in the bay and 500 horses tied in the woods.[159] This religious gathering was hailed at the time as "the largest that ever assembled in Cape Breton."[160] In fact, it probably set a Canadian record.[161]

Mira's communions continued to draw large crowds like a magnet throughout the 1850s. In 1855, some 5–6,000 gathered at "The Ferry" and the following year, the audience reputedly numbered 8,000.[162] Although gradually tapering off, these extraordinary figures were still reported in the 1860s through the 1890s. For example, Whycocomagh's sacramental season

in 1865 boasted some 5,000 worshippers, although some ob-
servers gauged the numbers as high as 7,000.[163] In July 1871,
a gathering of 5–6,000 assembled at Mira's communion. The
same number was quoted for Mira's sacramental services in
September 1890 and September 1892.[164] Of course, there was
also an ample number of clergy on hand at this event. The
host minister could not handle such hordes by himself. He
was usually assisted by at least one or two neighbouring clerics along with an invited minister, typically a distinguished
speaker, whose preaching talents had star power.

It is recorded that by ten o'clock the communion site was
filled with people shaking hands and exchanging salutations
with friends and relatives. The social interaction, Farnham
observed, was subdued and sober-faced. There were no
conspicuous demonstrations of affection: "sisters even did
not kiss."[165] The crowd that congregated on the grounds was
invariably a "mixed gathering," comprising a wide spectrum
of saints and sinners; the latter lumped by the Rev. Alexander
Ross into the category of "nominal Protestants ... practical
infidels" whose church-going was often limited to the sacramental gatherings.[166] Along with the godly were those more
worldly-minded who had "evidently come because others
were coming—to see and to be seen."[167] Nevertheless, before
the Sabbath service began, even those who had congregated
for primarily recreational reasons, exhibited a respectable decorum and much of the conversation was "low voiced talk."[168]
For the Rev. Dr. Masson of Edinburgh, the scene he witnessed
at Boularderie's communion Sunday in 1872 moved him pro-
foundly. As he surveyed the crowd of 1,200 people, his eyes
wandering slowly from face to face, his memory recorded this
snapshot view:

> What a sight: grandsires of eighty winters and the youth
> of scarce twelve summers; strong men in their prime and
> graceful maidens in their teens; here a clump of old men,
> head bare of bonnet and protecting locks, each leaning on
> his staff, eager for the word of life; and there a line of aged
> women, mutch covered with handerchief, and the black
> shawl, with one hand, held up to the angle of the mouth, as
> they rocked to and fro, and wept with deep emotion....[169]

The attire of the worshippers during the sacramental season was also noteworthy. Outsiders were always struck by the predominance of black. The communion was not a showcase for sartorial splendour; there was a definite communion-season clothing code during the mid-19th century. It was not, for example, the appropriate occasion to debut one's new paisley shawl.[170] In fact, the communion-season clothing code during the mid-19th century dictated that both men and women dress sombrely without adornment or colour.[171] One summer visitor to Cape Breton in 1841 remarked on the virtual absence of women's bonnets at these early gatherings.[172] During the late 1830s and early 1840s, the only bonnets to be found on Boularderie Island belonged to the wives of the Rev. James Fraser, the first settled Presbyterian minister at Boularderie, and Alexander Munro, the local schoolmaster.[173] The Rev. Alexander Farquharson noted that the majority of the female members in his Middle River congregation wore cotton handkerchiefs as their preferred style of headdress; his wife and three other ladies resplendent in their bonnets were the conspicuous exception. For Farquharson, it was lamentable that after the first communion service was held in Middle River in 1838, "the bonnets came in by the dozen!"[174] The men, as a rule, were attired in trousers and short jackets made of coarse blue woolen cloth with a lavender-coloured cast. Collars and coats were seldom worn.[175] By the mid 1860s, a delegation of visiting clergy confirmed the continued prevalence of homespun and the scarcity of broadcloth.[176] They were also struck by the fact that the participants were not "tricked out in the newest style."[177] The men were bareheaded, while the young women wore modest "cottage bonnets," with neatly strapped ribbons.[178] The predominant headdress of the older women was a white frilled muslin cap covered with a black handkerchief. The black shawl was worn by women of all ages. Clearly, understatement and modesty in style of dress were the order of the day. Sometimes a modicum of material vanity was subtly exhibited as the young girls in their kerchiefs, a triangular piece of cloth called a *soiltean*, "vied with one another as to who would have the most neatly hemmed."[179]

During his visit to Cape Breton in 1885, Charles Farnham witnessed a similar scene of black straw sunbonnets, black kerchiefs and black shawls. Other travel accounts reveal that he was not alone in his overwhelming impression of austerity and plainness in the worshippers' attire. Charles Dudley Warner, also an American writer, volunteered an explanation, rationalizing that their simplicity of dress was merely the outward manifestation of rigid Scots Presbyterianism.[180] Perhaps, he was not far off the mark. According to cultural historian Philippe Perrot, the abandonment of display and colour in fashion, essentially an act of negation, signifies a value system with propriety, reserve, self-control, conformity, self-denial, thrift and merit as its main ethical components.[181] He also states that church-going attire in the 19th century was regulated by Western fashion imperatives which stipulated modesty, or rather "conspicuous underconsumption" in dress, as the appropriate expression of Christian humility; although contemporary sermon and manual writers lead one to suspect that more "showy costumes" were the norm.[182]

Clearly, the prevailing style of dress at the Cape Breton Presbyterian communions had another significance. The ubiquitous black and negligible differences in the garb of various social classes and of the young and older women reflected and reinforced the communal aspect of the sacramental season. It was a time when social distinctions were suspended. Within such a context, clothing was not meant to affirm class hierarchies and divisions; instead, sameness in dress was an expression of solidarity, uniformity and homogeneity.

The actual physical setting of the open-air communions was charged with meaningful symbolism.[183] During the sacramental seasons in the Scottish Highlands, for example, parishioners gathered in the open air, usually in a deep romantic "dell," a locality deemed analogous to the site of the original "tabernacle in the wilderness."[184] The same formula was used in Cape Breton. "The Ferry" on the Mira River was regarded as the ideal communion site. It was situated in a sheltered glen at the head of a small bay, and the level green tract where the worshippers congregated was enclosed by overarching spruce and juniper trees.[185] The location afforded a spectacular vista of "green banks, wooded isles, headlands and coves."[186] Not only could this spot accommodate thousands, it was also "remarkably well adapted for sitting and hearing."[187] In such a majestic and evocative setting, the participants were overcome by the conviction that they were performing a primaeval ritual that savoured of the eternal and were breaking the crust of the holy bread for the first time. They were urged to revel in their natural setting, to remember the Ark in the wilderness and to envisage Abraham, Isaac and Jacob and the "other ancient patriarchs, who laid their victims on the unhewn rock for an altar, and burnt their incense under the shade of a green tree."[188] These were stimulating thoughts and the setting at Mira, filled with the lingering fragrance of summer, fed the senses and the emotions. These locations, however humble and rustic, were elevated to the status of "temples of nature," embowered sanctuaries of solace, inspiration and celebration.[189]

At Whycocomagh, the open-air services were conducted on a hillside, sheltered from the wind by a thick barrier of trees. As if designed for this express purpose, the hill resembled both in form and acoustic properties a natural amphitheatre. Moreover, its proximity to Loch Bras d'Or heightened its symbolic appeal.[190] The "feast on the grass near the Lake" was redolent of "that other Feast, held nearly nineteen hundred years ago on the east side of the Sea of Galilee."[191] The simplicity of this environment conveyed a majestic purity and elemental beauty which accentuated the supernatural character of the Sàcramaid. Describing the Whycocomagh open-air communion, the Rev. D. McMillan exclaimed: "no service in a Gothic cathedral was ever more impressive."[192]

Similar principles operated at other communion sites. For example, a "beautiful" amphitheatre-shaped "nook" near the harbour accommodated St. Ann's summer Sàcramaid,[193] while a "sweet, bosky dell," set against a sloping hillside, sufficed as the venue for Broad Cove's sacramental season.[194] The West Bay congregation held its open-air service in a "beautiful glen" cleared of underbrush and sheltered by large trees.[195] At Boulardrie, the Lord's Supper was staged in a "lovely hol-

Fig. 11 Late 19th-century communion service at Mira, NS. Reprinted with permission of Union Presbyterian Church, Mira Ferry.

low encompassed by trees" while at Middle River, a "beautiful grove" of maples and elms served the purpose.[196] These sylvan trysting places with God had a spiritual as well as poetic power. Over time, they became vested with occult significance. They were sanctified by "many a precious season" and for some worshippers became the cherished sites of their own "spiritual Israels," where they had "received the first impressions of religion, and [where] Christ made himself known to their souls."[197] For example, the Rev. Murdoch Buchanan, inducted in 1900 as Louisbourg's first regularly settled minister, traced his epiphanic experience and spiritual conversion to a sacramental gathering at St. Ann's. Communion-goers frequently ascribed superior mystical power to certain locales in Cape Breton, deemed special "sacred spaces" where contact with God was assured.[198] Among the members of the South Gut congregation, the "Glen" near "old Murdoch Buchanan's Barn" enjoyed this rarefied status. In 1905, *The Blue Banner* reported: "It is stated and reverently believed that here God has been pleased to pour out upon the people of His spirit—no small measure. It is certainly true that to this novel service the people flock in larger numbers than elsewhere."[199]

Fig. 12 The "tent" at Whycocomagh, NS. c.1930s
Photo by: Clara Dennis, Reprinted with
permission of NSARM. No 387 Clara Dennis
Collection- Cape Breton 1981- 541/387.

Fig. 13 The "tent" at
Boularderie, NS, c.1940s.
Reprinted with permission

There was something strangely atavistic about Cape Breton's open-air tradition. After all, had not the Romans and Greeks enshrined groves as favourite places for worship, believing them to be sacred because they were haunted by gods? Many communion-goers in Cape Breton were wedded to this open-air tradition, preferring the sward to the pew, the unbroken forest to whitewashed walls, the canopy of sky and spruce to a wooden roof and spire.[200] The "old men & women," in particular, were fond of this natural setting, preferring to meet outside even when the weather was inclement.[201] One elder insisted to his minister that "he could hear a great deal better in the open air than in the church"; although the Rev. Ross noted cynically, "[He] had been pretty deaf for a number of years."[202] The reverential attitude towards the tradition of outdoor worship may very well have had a decisive impact on Cape Breton's unique ecclesiastical architecture. According to Susan Hyde and Michael Bird, authors of *Hallowed Timbers*, Cape Breton's wooden churches, with their stirring vistas of water and forest and simplicity of sacred form, are imbued with a "sense of the transcendent with a reverence for nature."[203]

The Sabbath service usually began at 11 a.m., although communions earlier in the 19th century commenced at 10:30. The English-speaking worshippers repaired to a nearby church or barn for separate services, while the Gaelic speakers congregated outdoors near the "tent," a species of pulpit. Originally a Highland tradition, the "tent" was a moveable booth-like structure which sheltered officiating clergy, sometimes numbering as many as four. It was a plain, utilitarian construction, often left out in the elements year-round.[204] Within this roofed enclosure (either peaked or rounded) with its wide open window, the ministers sat on an uncushioned bench.[205] Several printed sources indicate that the "tent" also housed a desk and had a hinged window that lifted up.[206] Although modest, this building with its raised floor functioned as a dais, focusing attention on the ministers and signifying their honoured position in the Sabbath service. During the early years of Cape Breton's sacramental seasons, the "tent" was simply a makeshift canopy fashioned from canvas. By 1855, Whycocomagh boasted "the best of the kind in Cape Breton."[207] Fortunately, more specific details have survived about the "new tent" purchased by Boularderie's Presbyterian church in 1891 for $28.00. It measured twelve feet square with doors placed at each end for ventilation.[208] The Sacrament tent at Baddeck Forks, used until 1910, had its own distinctive features and was described as follows:

> The Minister enters the TENT by a Dutch-door on the left side: the top panel is usually left open for air. Opposite the door is a small sliding panel: this regulates the draft. Along the back end of the Tent is a bench. At the front end of this stall is a large unglazed window; and it is through this aperture that the preacher thrusts his head and shoulders.[209]

The tents must have been a tight squeeze for some clergy, especially for the likes of the Rev. Alexander Farquharson who was a stout six foot two.[210]

In front of the tent, directly below the preacher, was positioned the precentor, who usually stood on a platform. Nearby were situated one or two long narrow trestle tables covered with white linen. The communion table used at West Bay's summer Sàcramaid in 1864 allegedly extended forty to fifty feet.[211] The table at Loch Lomond was smaller, approximately twenty-five to thirty feet.[212] Along each side were several low rough benches strategically placed so that the communicants faced each other. Installed nearby were several posts or stumps fitted with small collection boxes for the reception of offerings, popularly known as the "Copper Collection." At later communions, a more extensive assortment of benches was also in evidence.[213]

The furnishings at the open-air communions were simple to the extreme. The seating arrangements of the worshippers were much more complex. Occupying the "space of honour" close to the tent were the flint-faced elders and precentors with sunburned necks, weathered visages and out-thrust bearded chins.[214] They were ensconced there, as one observer noted, "as if this were their place by right, and by the courteous consent of the reverential younglings all around them."[215] Some among this saintly band sat on chairs, others rested on the grass, often leaning on their staffs. Seated beside this elite group were their wives, the women often dubbed "Mothers in Israel."[216] The rest of the worshippers fanned out from there, sitting bolt upright on the grass or perching on convenient stumps or stones. Physical comfort was not a priority; no one dared succumb to the temptation to recline.

The positioning of worshippers was far from random. It made tangible a myriad of cleavages based on age as well as states of grace. The young and the old "kept pretty distinct" with the elderly congregated nearest to the tent.[217] This privileged location was also occupied by the communicants while those of "lesser degrees of piety made concentric circles there-about," fanning out, seated on the hillside, tier upon tier, upward and around.[218] At the furthest edge of the gathering were the carriages, wagons, carts and horses, tethered to trees or fence posts.

The audience at the open-air communion constituted a fascinating microcosm of community life. One's seating location reflected the dichotomies between young and old as well as between communicants and adherents, for only the "experienced saints" were planted in close proximity to the tent.[219] These distinctions were even more sharply drawn at Black River in 1914. There the communicants were allocated seats specially installed in front and on each side of the tent.[220] The moral scenery at Cape Breton's open-air communions revealed yet a third division, a linguistic-based distinction; the outdoor communion was conducted almost exclusively in Gaelic, while English-speaking worshippers convened in a nearby church or barn for separate services.

The outdoor communion service in Cape Breton invariably commenced with psalms and prayers. These served as a prelude to the all-important "Action Sermon," an animated address disclosing the central truths of redemption, delivered by one of the ministers in the tent. During the mid- to late-19th century, these sermons—memorized or extemporaneous—were highly charged and evangelical. Scottish Presbyterians tended to look askance at ministers who slavishly read their prepared texts. Farnham was particularly struck by the preacher's style of delivery with its characteristic long pauses, whining repetition, "majestic slowness" and a slow rocking movement from side to side.[221]

For Cape Breton ministers, it was their "performance" at the communion services that sealed their reputations as preachers and divines, for the Word at these gatherings was "preached" as well as "performed."[222] The preaching style of the Gaelic-speaking ministers was characterized by several distinctive hallmarks. As the ministers engaged in a "swaying motion," they delivered their evangelical message in "pleading" tones that were reminiscent of a "whine" or "sough."[223] Ac-cording to Canadian religious historian, John Grant, this technique was far more effective in Gaelic and was "not easily transferred to English."[224] Outsiders were invariably struck by the novelty of the rocking movement which, according to one witness, "seemed essential to all these Cape Breton speakers and singers."[225]

The Rev. Peter McLean, one-time minister at Whycocomagh, was renowned for moving communion-season listeners to tears, with a voice that was vigorous and symphonious, reaching the distant corners of his audience. [226] In fact, McLean's powers as a Gaelic preacher were considered unparalleled among many Cape Breton congregations.[227] McLean generated such a devoted following that people flocked to hear him, "eagerly" following "him from place to place."[228] His demonstrative revivalist style of preaching moulded the faith of many mid-19th-century Cape Breton Presbyterians. It was not uncommon practice for obituaries to include some formulaic reference to McLean as an instrument of God in the spiritual destiny of the deceased.[229]

The Rev. Dr. Hugh McLeod was also a celebrated preacher throughout Cape Breton. His legacy was a vast one. McLeod was wont to boast that he had preached during his career nearly 4,000 sermons, baptized about 900 persons, married several hundred couples, admitted to the communion of the church about 600 people and distributed 2,000 copies of scripture and many thousand tracts "chiefly gratuitously."[230] His real forte was addressing the vast Gaelic congregations at the outdoor communions and in his prime he was without peer.[231] With his forceful and plain depictions of sin and God's love, he held the attention of his God-fearing audience, from the first sentence to the last. There was eager anticipation when the "Doctor" was slated to give the "action sermon." He was regarded as the "prince of preachers" and people expected something grand, edifying and stirring.[232] According to the *Presbyterian Witness*, "We have not heard anywhere a preacher who could hold a vast audience more thoroughly under his control than Dr. Macleod.... It is no exaggeration to say that thousands hung with rapture on his words."[233] His charisma as a preacher was further heightened by his physical attributes. McLeod's eyes were piercing and his forehead was expansive so that in "face and form and feature, he is emphatically a strong man."[234] Judging from published accounts, McLeod's sermon oratory was "intensively realistic," highly evangelical and metaphorical.[235] His clear, pealing voice and emphatic style of expression projected great vigour, and he strove deliberately to excite the spiritual passions of his listeners. He would stir them into a swaying movement reminiscent of trees convulsed by a gale. According to one of his colleagues, he "used to push on till the strong crying of the people stopped him."[236] On one famous occasion, during the revival of 1870, a weeping congregation actually forced McLeod to halt in the middle of his sermon and resume only after the singing of a psalm pacified them.[237] Clearly, McLeod pitched his reverberant message to his listeners' emotions rather than to their minds by drawing them into the dynamic realm of sensation.

Not all the Presbyterian clergy in Cape Breton conformed to McLeod's signature style of preaching. Although evangelical in his Free Church sympathies, the Rev. Matthew Wilson of Sydney Mines was much more restrained in his manner of presentation. His sermons demonstrated "fine rhetorical method"and a scholarly choice of language.[238] Then again, this Lowlander was not a Gaelic preacher. It was McLeod's preaching technique, not Wilson's, that became the *beau-idéal* at Cape Breton's 19th-century communions. Other preachers, such as the Scottish-born Rev. John Rose, were also deeply evangelical. One-time minister of Whycocomagh (1884-1892) and later Malagawatch and River Denys (1896-1909), he too capped his reputation as a Gaelic preacher at Cape Breton's open-air communions. It is recorded in the Presbytery of Inverness minutes: "He was, perhaps, at his best when addressing his fellow Highlanders on Communion Season in the open air, and impressions made will not soon be forgotten."[239]

The key to the magnetic appeal of many of Cape Breton's 19th-century preachers, especially those who excelled at Gaelic oratory, went much deeper than personal attributes. Their homiletic style tapped into a cultural context where oral transmission was central and the sermon and the folktale shared a "common ground."[240] In the Gaelic-speaking Highlands, the sermon was essentially an "oral artifact" delivered without a prepared text and in a manner which bore a striking conformity to the "indigenous chant used to transmit Gaelic heroic ballads"; this mode of delivery, as noted in *The Dictionary of Scottish Church History & Theology*, was well-suited to the physical demands of open-air preaching.[241] The Gaelic sermon with its staple messages of consolation, counsel and caution was also replete with exempla, a common preaching tool designed to drive home a moral teaching.[242] Such an illustrative device helped firmly implant the ministers' discourses in the minds and memories of his listeners. Little wonder that the words that fell from the lips of some of Cape Breton's Gaelic-speaking clergy became part of a shared oral tradition to be summoned "from memory whenever a conversation called for spiritual edification."[243]

Cape Breton Presbyterians were notorious for their stamina during this marathon of sermons. Worshippers at mid-19th century communions were attentive for hours on end, not easily distracted by the commotion of the late-comers, or the impatient neighing of the horses. Some pored over Bibles, assiduously marking passages mentioned by the preacher. Such earnest deportment had not always been the norm. One Cape Breton cleric, who arrived in the 1830s, had found his audiences restless and inattentive, their eyes wandering "hither and thither, and the word seemed to produce no effect."[244] During one sermon, he had to stop several times to rebuke them. Two decades later, he was struck by their transformation: "But now the eye is fixed, the attention arrested, and the hearted melted."[245]

Despite the old saw that "ministers and sacraments make bad weather," rain and wind did not dampen the spiritual fervour of most Cape Breton Presbyterians.[246] At Whycocomagh's communion in September 1860, worshippers remained at the Sabbath service until shortly after five o'clock despite torrential rain.[247] At an open-air communion at Strathlorne in August 1872, participants sat in the incessant rain for two hours. One witness marvelled: "For five hours and twenty minutes that multitude sat upon the soaking grass as if glued to it."[248] There is no easy explanation for their high threshold of tolerance for such discomforts. It was a testament to their ruggedness, the tenacity of tradition and "the absorbing sincerity of their piety."[249] One cleric attributed it to Scottish practicality—that after having travelled so far to hear sermons, Highlanders "like to get a good deal for their trouble."[250] But this appetite for sermons had little to do with stereotypical frugality. It signified the central importance of preaching to Highland worshippers, especially in a sacramental context, where the sermon offered "prayerful stimulation" toward a union with

Christ.[251] The Word and the Sacrament were fundamentally connected: "for the right celebration of the Sacrament the Word was necessary."[252]

Cape Breton Presbyterians were also renowned for their exacting standards for preaching. The Rev. D. B. Blair of Barney's River found them extremely discriminating listeners. "They are not," he wrote, "easily satisfied with everything that is presented to them in the shape of preaching. It will not do to send either a Boy or a Booby to preach to such people."[253] The Rev. John Neil of Toronto made a similar observation, noting that they would "not tolerate poor preaching." To his amazement, he discovered that Cape Breton's Gaelic-speaking Presbyterians scorned translated English sermons masquerading as Gaelic. Linguistic pride, Neil concluded, accounted for their insistence that "they will not have an English sermon warmed over in a Gaelic oven, but their spiritual food must be kneaded by Gaelic hands, baked over a Gaelic fire, before it will be acceptable to a Gaelic taste."[254]

Fig. 14 Commemorative re-enactment of a traditional Scottish open-air communion, Union Presbyterian Church, Mira Ferry, 1975, Reprinted with permission of Bill Morrison. Centre standing, Rev. Everett H. Bean with servers Bill Morrison (Marion Bridge) and Robert Ferguson (Glace Bay). Also in attendance Jordan MacMillan (Catalone), Rev. Angus MacKinnon (Glace Bay), Rev. M. MacRae (Boularderie), Dan Matheson (Dutch Brook), Neil MacDonald (Sydney) and Donald Cameron (Louisbourg).

The Communion

After the "action sermon," the celebration of the Lord's Supper followed, prefaced by the stern caveats of the minister in the "fencing of the tables." This segment of the service consisted of a scrutinizing commentary on the godly and the godless, inviting one to the Lord's Table while debarring the other. Among those banished from this ordinance were Sabbath-breakers, drunkards, gossips, unfit parents, disobedient children and the earthly-minded.

While the congregation sang a psalm, the communicants advanced tentatively with the minister's stark warnings in their ears, gaining admission by depositing their tokens on a plate held by one of the elders.[255] With mingled awe and gladness, these "poor wrestling souls" approached with the demeanour of those who had deliberated with much thought and prayer and were sobered by the prospect of performing the "most solemn business that can be transacted on earth."[256] After blessing the elements, the minister then came down from the "tent" and addressed those seated on the hard benches. He urged them as "heirs of heaven" to contemplate their wretched state of sin while partaking the "Gospel feast."[257] The goblet of wine and the plate of bread were then delivered to the elders who gravely passed them along "that very long table."[258] The communicants sat silently, down-cast and solemn-faced, in penitent poses; the women's heads were draped with black shawls. The face-to-face seated posture of the participants at the table was "a forceful symbol of a community feasting together."[259]

Even as they strained to catch a glimpse of the proceedings, for those people seated along the rim of the audience, it must have been difficult to follow the subtleties of the service. Angus Hector MacLean, for example, later confessed that at his first communion he was surprised to discover that the "sacred bread" was not "some uniquely fancy kind of bread," but resembled "a plate of mother's bread broken up for the chickens."[260] And yet, during the actual dispensation of communion, a hush reputedly would fall over the audience as they watched. It was an "eloquent" stillness signifying a collective sense that this was a transcendent moment, in and out of time: "God was in this place ... how it was none other than the house of God—how it was the gate of heaven."[261] Even the youths who lurked "on the outskirts of the congregation" were seen standing "in awe for that time."[262]

All eyes were trained on those people who were bold enough to venture first to the Lord's Table. During the heyday of the temperance movement, even the zeal with which certain communicants quaffed the wine was closely monitored: "Anyone who raised his head and tossed it back would be noted."[263] It is difficult to estimate how much wine was used at Cape Breton communions. According to American historian, Leigh Schmidt, wine flowed copiously at Pennsylvania's mid-18th century sacraments. He estimates that each communicant consumed approximately four ounces of wine.[264] On mainland Nova Scotia, New Annan's sacramental gathering in July 1860 required one and one-quarter gallons of wine; the previous year "a keg of wine" had sufficed.[265] Unfortunately, the Kirk Session records for Cape Breton fail to provide any detailed account of expenditures for wine. Still, it is clear that as the temperance movement swept across Cape Breton, communicants were permitted little more than an imperceptible sip from the goblet.

After the elements were dispensed, the communicants listened to a second "table" address, an exhortation to embrace model Christian lives and to give witness. This was no casual admonition—the words could be intimidating. The worshippers sat still, in respectful contemplation of God's judgment, with its grim overtones of hellfire and sulphur. The Rev. Matthew Wilson dismissed his communicants in August 1872 with this chastening message:

> Your vows have been recorded in heaven—Oh! Then see to it that you perform them: for God has no pleasure in them that vow and perform not: and if you have not so vowed, what have you been doing, and what has induced you to come to the Sacrament?[266]

The Rev. Hugh McLeod's words were no less daunting and uncompromising. In addition to reminding communicants of their solemn pledge to make Christ "the business of your lives," he warned them against relapses and alerted them to the stratagems of Satan. Satan, he exclaimed, "is never more busy than after a Sacrament," lying in wait "for your soul communicant when you leave the banqueting house."[267] Little wonder, participants returned solemnly to their respective places, "deeply sensible of their responsibility to God for the privileges they enjoyed."[268]

Since communion was conducted in relays, preparations were then made for the next table service. Even at this sacred climax in the Sabbath service, linguistic distinctions were preserved. At some sacramental gatherings, the English-speaking participants took communion in the church. In other instances, they were served separately in the open-air. For example, there were individual sittings for both English and Gaelic speakers at Big Baddeck's open-air communion in the fall of 1869. It is interesting to note that precedence was accorded the Gaelic communicants, for their table was invariably served first; although with multiple sittings, they often alternated as required.[269]

In the overall drama of Cape Breton's outdoor communions, the precentors were far from bit players. They enjoyed top billing, their status second in importance only to the preachers. Much-respected members of the church, they single-handedly controlled the musical part of public worship in the Presbyterian church for most of the 19th century. The precenting tradition of Gaelic metrical psalms had venerable origins. This form of musical praise harkened back to the Scottish Reformation when the use of musical instruments in churches came under heavy censure. Although the evolutionary development of Highland-precented singing is "historically obscure," the tradition had particular relevance for Cape Breton's Presbyterian pioneers for whom printed hymn and psalm books were in short supply.[270] The precentor's box, a railed enclosure, occupied a privileged position in the church, outrivaled only by the minister's pulpit. At the open air communion, the precentor stood in front of the tent, just below the preacher. His primary task was to "give out the line," that is to lead the congregation in song by intoning (usually reading then singing) the psalm line by line.[271] The end result was a highly individuated performance, a singular acoustic blending of "the congregation's individual response to the melody and the individual precentor's leading."[272]

At the open-air communions, no musical instruments were tolerated and worshippers revelled in the precentor's familiar melodies which resonated throughout the crowd. The psalms were sung to traditional tunes popular among the Highlanders, many of them secular in nature, such as "Bangor," "Coleshill (sometimes called the Communion tune),""Dundee,""St. David's,""Elgin,""Evan,""Kilmarnock," "New London,""Duke Street,""St. Ann,""Balerma,""Jackson," "French," "St. Andrew," "Eastgate," "St. Paul," "Irish" and "Martyrdom."[273] The choice of tunes was far from random and was predicated on a congregation's specific preferences. In fact, throughout Cape Breton, there were many permutations of precenting practices, with unique elements shaped by local customs and the distinctive styles of precentors.[274]

This singular musical form had many memorable characteristics. The tempo was slow, accented by "extended intonations with numerous slurs," culminating in crescendos.[275] At times, the tune, so layered with ornamental flourishes and drawn-out passages, was barely recognizable. To the outsider, this unaccompanied singing, which possessed an alien, otherwordly quality, sounded more like wailing or chanting; "more Hindoo than Anglo Saxon," was how Ruth Kedzie Wood described it in her book, *The Tourist's Maritime Provinces,* published in 1915.[276]

Those who practised the "specialized art" of precenting were revered as an important part of Presbyterian Scottish culture.[277] Their voices were important musical leaven not only to communions, but also to funerals and prayer meetings. In East Lake Ainslie, Big Farquhar MacKinnon enchanted audiences with his precenting as well as his "expert" bagpiping. He left an indelible impression on Archie MacPhail of Scotsville who recalled: "He'd hold the book with both hands, and his big fingers would be going up and down on the covers as if playing the pipes."[278] At Marion Bridge, Donald John Lamond, one-time elder at the Scotch Presbyterian Church in Boston, was regarded as one of the region's most gifted Gaelic precentors; he returned to the Mira in 1902 and continued to precent well into his 90s.[279] The "sweet" melodious voice of Charles Campbell, born in Coll, led the Malagawatch congregation singing in both English and Gaelic for more than sixty years, until his death in 1910.[280] The senior elder at Leitches Creek, A. R. McDonald, who was born in 1829, was also a tireless Gaelic precentor, serving his congregation for forty years. According to the records of the Presbytery of Sydney, "He led in the singing of the songs of Zion in the sanctuary services and in the cottage assemblings for prayer in his district from the days when his locks were like the raven until long after they were like snow…. He loved the songs of Zion and helped others to love them."[281]

Infused with inspirational words and music, the Sabbath communion service was a highly emotional event. Sources indicate that Cape Breton's 19th-century sacramental seasons often produced an intense spiritual rapture. In fact, the Lord's Supper served as the focal point of many revivals and became a potent instrument for enhancing religious feeling and personal conversion. The accounts of weeping, loud cries, rocking movements and prostration call into question the stereotype of the dour, undemonstrative Scot. At Mira's first communion in August 1852, tears flowed profusely. The following summer, the response was even more pronounced:

> The arrows of conviction flew thick amongst them, and not only was serious look, grave deportment, and weeping eyes seen in all directions, but, also more unmistakeable indications of deep distress. Thousands were melted. Many cried out in the bitterness of their soul. Some of both sexes trembled under the Word, and in a variety of ways manifested deep feeling.[282]

Such thrilling scenes were not limited to Mira's sacramental gatherings. At the communion at Sydney Mines in August 1853, "deep feeling" was registered with tears and "bitter cries."[283] One of the most striking and salient features of this spiritual outpouring was the youthfulness of its participants. On this point, the Rev. Hugh McLeod wrote: "It is pleasing to observe that, although not confined to them, yet the movement is principally among the young—especially the young men, and in some instances, the most unlikely in point of character."[284] The Rev. Peter McLean also detected this generational bias, noting "Scarcely a young man but carries a Gaelic psalm book in his pocket where ever he goes, not a young woman without one in her bosom."[285]

Accounts from the 1870s are even more melodramatic. The Rev. James F. Campbell was amazed by the outburst of emotion he witnessed at Broad Cove Intervale during the summer of 1872: "Strong men, from whom it could take much to wring a tear in public, gazed at the preachers with moistened eyes; not women only, but men rocked to and from, and tears and sobs, groans and even piercing cries burst from many."[286] At the Mira communion in July 1870, there was an overpowering reaction. At the Monday service, after the minister delivered some parting words, there were "cries of mercy, which might be heard at a considerable distance. Several were prostrated and could not leave the place for some time."[287] Some people eventually had to be led away. That summer, the responses at the Boularderie and Sydney Mines communions (where the Gaelic service was conducted in the churchyard) were equally compelling. The Rev. Hugh McLeod recorded the following account:

> We were scarcely half through with the discourse when the whole congregation seemed to be in tears, and then gave vent to their feelings, by crying bitterly in great distress. The scene was extremely solemn, and so overpowering that it was impossible to proceed. We had to pause, sing and pray two or three times. It was the same on Monday.[288]

Unfortunately, few detailed descriptions of Cape Breton's Presbyterian revival during the early 1870s survive. During this decade, the revivalistic spirit quickened the pulse of religiosity throughout Cape Breton's Presbyterian congregations as audiences were overcome with a sense of humankind's sin and depravity, the necessity of repentance and regeneration, the dangers of delay, the fullness of Christ's atonement and the holiness, sovereignty and justice of God. The message about sins and souls was an overwhelming one. One woman phrased it thus:"she could no more stand against it, than a fly would stand before the lightning."[289] Among the awakened were children under fourteen, people over sixty, but by far the most numerous were between the ages of twenty and thirty. The Rev. Hugh McLeod claimed that "in some cases whole families have been hopefully converted. In others entire hamlets, consisting of several families."[290] In his estimation, Cape Breton's spiritual awakening compared favourably to similar movements abroad:

> I have seen much of the Lord's work in Ross-shire and other parts of Scotland, in Ireland, and in the United States, but I must say, that in no congregation have I seen anything so general, so deep, and so thorough, as I now see within my own charge here.[291]

The elders at St. John's Presbyterian Church in Port Morien were also heartened by the changes in their own membership, especially the widespread transformation in moral behaviour. The Session minutes noted: "Many who were accustomed to be in the 'Drinking Saloon' on former New Years were now in their right mind and sitting at the Lord's table."[292]

Only a fraction of those who attended the communion season actually approached the table on the Sabbath. For example, at the ceremony held at Boularderie in August 1839, approximately 60 of a total of 2,000 participated, while during the Whycocomagh communion of 1855 attended by 4,500 worshippers, 200 communicants were recorded.[293] In the Rev. Abraham McIntosh's congregation of 180 families in St. Ann's and North Shore, there were only 8 communicants recorded in 1857; that same year the Rev. James Fraser's Boularderie congregation of 200 had no more than 50 communicants.[294] The figures were equally dismal for the Rev. Kenneth McKenzie's Baddeck congregation in 1858 which consisted of 133 families and only 8 communicants, although 350 people regularly attended public worship.[295]

Following the practice of their Free Church counterparts in Scotland, the mid-19th-century Cape Breton Presbyterian clergy exercised stiff fencing procedures. Participants were chastised about "trampling" the Sàcramaid as an "unholy thing" and warned that "he that eateth and drinketh unworthily eateth and drinketh damnation to himself."[296] Inhibited by such caveats, people drew back in horror, convinced of their own unworthiness and fearful of incalculable injury to their souls.

This pattern was briefly interrupted in the early 1870s, during a period of intense revival activity. In January 1871, the minister in Cow Bay reported that within a year, the number of communicants had soared from 10 to 85.[297] He recalled with enthusiasm that "On that Communion Sabbath we saw, what we never witnessed before, three, four, five, and even six members of the same family at the Lord's table."[298] One mother with her three sons had communed for the first time, and another mother had sat at the Lord's Table with her three sons and two daughters. Similar responses were reported in other communities throughout the island. In 1871, Mira's communion roll increased by more than one-third and Sydney's more than doubled.[299] During the latter part of the 19th century, the percentage of Presbyterian communicants in Cape Breton continued to grow, but only gradually. The traditional timidity associated with sitting at the Lord's Table lingered. As late as 1904, the Presbytery of Sydney estimated a ratio of slightly more than one communicant per family; in at least seven congregations there were more families than communicants.[300] Local church officials regarded these statistics as disheartening, for they did not correlate with the Canadian norm.

Throughout the 19th century, the majority of those who came forward to the Lord's Table were "older persons, and well aged."[301] Some of the clergy found the widespread reticence discouraging. In 1865, it was mournfully reported that the proportion of communicants to the vast concourse of 5,000 to 7,000 at Whycocomagh "was so small as to be melancholy."[302] When the Rev. James Campbell attended the sacrament at Broad Cove Intervale in the summer of 1872, he was nonplussed by the sparse numbers of communicants: "Here were the 'fathers', but where were the 'little children' and the 'young men'?"[303] In August 1889, the clergy at Cape North grieved to see "so few of the young at the Lord's Table."[304] Such singular conduct struck outsiders as both perverse and inscrutable. The Anglican clergyman, the Rev. R. A. Arnold, was completely baffled by such attitudes and to his ecclesiastical superior reported that only nine communicants, all females, all Presbyterians, had attended his Easter Communion at Sydney Mines. "There is a strange backwardness among the flock in the observance of this ordinance," he wrote, "and tho' I have spoken often and plainly on the subject, yet hitherto it has had little effect."[305]

St. Ann's, the epitome of simple virtue and strict behaviour during the 19th century, stands out as the most extreme example of non-observance of the Lord's Supper in Cape Breton. The residents went more than thirty years without celebrating this rite during the stern pastorate of the Rev. Norman McLeod. Presiding over his congregation like some Old Testament prophet, McLeod deemed himself and his congregation too lowly to merit the exalted privilege of communion. In this context, he differed little from his austere Free Church contemporaries in the Hebrides who surrounded the Lord's Table with such "formidable ... hedges as made it an almost empty table."[306] St. Ann's waited until the settlement of the Rev. Abraham McIntosh in 1856 before the Lord's Supper was finally dispensed to its Presbyterian congregation.

Among the Presbyterian laity, the misgivings about coming forward to the table had little to do with complacency. Some clerics suspected less lofty reasons at work, blaming the prevalence of superstitious notions or the reluctance of worshippers to commit to the stringent criteria for holiness imposed on communicants by this sacred ordinance.[307] In short, they allegedly found the godly walk of life too straight and narrow for their tastes.

Other explanations, however, are more plausible. For example, many Scottish Presbyterians rated the Lord's Supper as a much more solemn ordinance than Baptism. In fact, they regarded the sacrament with an almost "terrified" awe.[308] The infrequency with which communion was celebrat-ed undoubtedly contributed to this heightened sense of significance which elevated the Lord's Supper to a loftier realm far beyond the everyday. Furthermore, the acute sense of disqualification among many potential communicants stemmed from a sense of their own unworthiness and the preciousness of the privilege.

There was also a pronounced age bias in the Highland communion tradition which regarded sitting at the Lord's Table as an honour belonging to the aged.[309] Among mid-19th-century Highlanders, even twenty-five was regarded as "a very early age at which to partake of the Lord's Supper."[310] When Neil MacOdrum, of Mira, in his mid-twenties became a communicant and shortly thereafter an elder, his elevation in status was greeted as a "rare thing," "an unheard of thing."[311] The other extreme also drew comment from the Presbyterian Witness which reported in September 1899 that one of the first-time communicants at Marion Bridge was actually eighty years old.[312] By the 20th century, popular wisdom still dictated that maturity and experience were requisite qualifications, that the "younger must be tried in the fiery furnace of life until, chastened and humbled" before receiving this high and holy privilege.[313] However, this age bias does not explain fully why legions of faultless and godly "aged men and women" abstained from communion. One suspects that the infrequent celebration of the Lord's Supper led to a magnified emphasis on its solemn and awful characteristics. But in other cases, another interesting phenomenon operated. Parishioners pr-actised a strange form of inverted snobbery, employing non-participation as a public statement of their piety. It was as though only the self-righteous and spiritually vain would be so presumptuous as to approach the communion table.[314]

Evidence suggests that taking communion, especially for the first time, was fraught with self-searching anguish. The Ceist expositions on genuine "tokens" of grace, the examinations for admission, the "fencing of the tables" and the pre- and post-Communion addresses cumulatively heightened this anxiety. They left people with an almost unattainable conception of salvation as a state beyond the reach of ordinary worshippers. Angus Hector MacLean re-called that he was in "a sad and baffled" frame of mind at his first communion.[315]

This situation worsened when he spied his parents holding back: "Most people did not think themselves good enough to take communion, and I knew Father and Mother thought so. What was I doing?"[316] For the Rev. Alexander Ross, a native of Wester Ross, Scotland, who ministered in Whycocomagh from 1894 to 1903, the occasion of his first communion induced symptoms of confusion and agitation, especially on the eve of the Sabbath service. Seeking guidance, he conferred with the elders and the clergy and battled with his conscience. "O what mental struggle! I knew it was my duty to go forward, but dread that I deceived myself and would be left to bring reproach upon the Redeemer's Cause."[317] Finally, he summoned courage to join the trickle of communicants to the last table. It had been a momentous and wrenching decision: "Had I not gone forward at that time, it is possible, I could never do so afterward."[318] For those individuals who passed up the opportunity to sit at the Lord's Table, there was also anguish. At the summer communion at St. Ann's in 1890, it was reported that "[s]ome at the close of the service, expressed their regret at not coming forward to commemorate their Saviour's dying love."[319]

Traditionally, the open-air Gaelic Sabbath communion service in Cape Breton ran at least five hours. During the serving of the "tables," which were filled and emptied two, three, four or more times, communicants were continually reminded of the gravity of their partaking of the sacraments, and the ceremony concluded with the "directions" of the minister, again exhorting the communicants to continue on the narrow path of morality and spirituality.[320] The service seldom drew to a close before 4:00 p.m. Much more typical were gatherings that finished by 4:30 or 5 p.m.[321] It is recorded that Boularderie's communion in 1839 concluded just short of 6 p.m. The long summer day then continued into the evening with fellowship and prayer.

Day of Thanksgiving

On Monday, the day of thanksgiving, there were usually services in both languages; the English service was held in the church while the Gaelic was delivered at the tent. The sermons on this day cautioned against the dangers of back-sliding. Between the services, a visitation of the congregation was occasionally held, during which the minister, elders and managers related details about the discharge of their duties.[322] After the Monday services, the Session usually concluded its official business, totalling the offerings collected over the five days and disbursing funds for wine and for the place-ment and removal of the tables. Other activities were often tack-ed onto the end of the day. At the close of the Monday thanksgiving service at Gabarus in August 1889, an Equal Rights Association was formed. Sometimes there was even a round of baptisms. According to historian Leigh Schmidt, the conjunction of the sacraments of baptism and the Lord's Supper during the communion season enhanced the richness of communal rituals, adding yet another dimension to the symbolic pilgrimage of faith.[323]

For the worshippers, the Monday "farewell service" was an emotional time. According to Mary and Nelena Patterson, who were interviewed in the early 1980s about Framboise's five-day communions, "It was sad, sad everybody used to cry."[324] Hence, the use of the term "Sad Day" in Whycocomagh.[325] No doubt, the women experienced mixed emotions, for they had to scramble to get caught up on the domestic chores set aside on the previous day. For those who were homebound, the re-turn trip afforded additional opportunities to socialize, mull over the scriptural truths revealed and to share news gleaned at the Sacrament. Meals were obtained en route without any cash exchanging hands, the currency of gossip was recom-pense enough. It is recorded that centenarian, Neil McIntosh of Framboise, during his two-day journey home on foot, made "several calls on friends and acquaintances on the way."[326] For Augusta McCurdy, a regular summer visitor to Cape Breton, the return trip from North River involved a terse exchange with an old farmer about the meaning of predestination. The conversation ended abruptly when she stated "'I am not a Presbyterian,' he looked me full in the face and very solemnly said 'Are you an infidel'?"[327] Post-communion travel did not end so happily for Catherine Chisholm heading home to

Brook Village from the sacrament at St. Ann's in September 1874. According to newspaper accounts, the bridge near Little Narrows collapsed under the weight of her carriage. The horse was bruised and the wagon broken to pieces, but efforts to save her proved futile as she was swept under by the current.[328]

For the clergy, Monday marked the end of an arduous five-day season crammed with religious activities. At South Gut, St. Ann's, in July 1891, there were no fewer than seventeen services held over the five-day period.[329] The demands of the sacramental season could take a serious physical toll on participants, especially on the clergy. In December 1857, the *Presbyterian Witness* reported that the Rev. W. G. Forbes, one-time minister at Port Hawkesbury, was still suffering the ill-effects of a "disorder … contracted by preaching in the open air."[330] Cape Breton's rugged terrain proved especially fatiguing for the Rev. Alexander Farquharson, who was renowned for his great bodily strength. During the nearly twenty-four years that he served the congregations of Lake Ainslie and Middle River, he carried leeches in his pocket as an antidote to relieve his feet often left sore and swollen from walking and standing. The Rev. Alexander Ross confessed that the punishing schedule of the communions left him "physically & mentally exhausted."[331] Normally he required several days to recuperate before heading off to the next communion; it was not uncommon for there to be three or four in close succession during the mid-19th century. Even the strong-framed body of the legendary Rev. Peter McLean was broken by the strains of toiling in the mission field of Cape Breton.[332] For weeks in succession he preached five days every week. In 1842, he returned to Scotland with dwindling energies, hoping to recover his health and missionary mettle. McLean's preaching agenda, during his historic visit to Cape Breton from Stornoway in 1866, vividly illustrates the hectic pace he maintained. During one sacramental season, he preached twice on Thursday, once on Friday and Saturday, twice on the Sabbath and again on Monday.[333] Certainly the sacramental season could be taxing, even for the spiritually fit.

Chapter Three

The Communion Season in Retreat

Despite the popularity of Cape Breton's open-air communions, by the first decade of the 20th century the tradition was in a state of flux and fragmentation. For example, the frequency of communions tended to increase. Some congregations staged them twice a year, others even quarterly.[1] Several Presbyterian congregations moved quite swiftly in this direction. As early as 1862, Sydney Mines started dispensing the Lord's Supper biannually.[2] By 1875, Sydney, Mira, Glace Bay and Port Morien also observed communion twice a year.[3] By 1902, even smaller communities such as Port Morien held the Sàcramaid three times a year.[4]

At the same time, changes in some congregations were more radical.[5] While out-door communions persisted in St. Ann's, Framboise, Catalone, Cleveland, Little Narrows, Boularderie, Loch Lomond and River Denys into the 20th century,[6] several communities took deliberate steps to cancel this sacramental custom; in the 1870s, Sydney Mines discontinued the practice altogether. During the late 1880s, Strathlorne adopted the new arrangement of administering the sacrament in the church only.[7] In the following decade, Middle River's communion was moved indoors, although the five-day format was retained.[8] By 1903, the congregation at Marion Bridge decided to have their Gaelic Communion service in the church.[9] Presbyterians in Ingonish reached the same decision by at least 1903;[10] Whycocomagh followed suit in 1905. In Loch Lomond, the annual outdoor Sàcramaid ceased with the construction of Calvin Presbyterian Church in 1910; Baddeck Forks held its last open-air sacrament that same year. Both St. Ann's and Boularderie held out much longer, until the early 1920s; Boularderie continued to celebrate the traditional long communion indoors until 1942. As communions were increasingly restricted to a church setting, communicants now sat in specially allocated pews draped with white cloths; the arrangement which still conveyed the symbolism of a special banquet was only a faint echo of the days when the rough-hewn communion tables were covered in snowy white linens.

Other churches innovated compromises in response to the growing demands of efficiency. *MacTalla* reported that in August 1894, all communion season services at Little Narrows, save for the Gaelic sacrament, were confined to the church.[11] In 1903, the Presbyterian congregation at Gabarus effected a strange reversal, staging Gaelic services, including communion, in the church, while English-speaking participants met at the "tent."[12] The same practice was adopted by the Boularderie congregation in 1907. The Session Minutes reveal that this decision was prompted by the dictates of time.[13] Glace Bay experimented with an even more unusual permutation. During its summer sacramental season of 1888, Gaelic worshippers were accommodated in the local Baptist church, while their English-speaking counterparts met in the Presbyterian church.[14]

Other changes were directed at the duration of the communion season, as some congregations at the turn of the century moved to abandon the "fast day" and the "day of thanksgiving."[15] By 1895, neither River Inhabitants nor Baddeck had Thursday or Monday services.[16] In these congregations, the preparatory service was usually held on Friday. The event was scaled down in other ways as well. In 1909, for example, the

Rev. Angus McMillan conducted all the communion season services at Marion Bridge by himself without the usual muster of fellow clergy at his side. In effect, the foreshortened communion season became a miniaturized re-enactment of the old tradition.

The familiar accoutrements of the outdoor communion also underwent modification. The mid-19th century sacrament had featured one table, thereby necessitating a succession of sittings, which prolonged the service. But, by the turn of the century, various kirk sessions agreed to enlarge table accommodations so that "one Table Service" would often suffice.[17] In August 1907, the Margaree Session, seeking a more "convenient" and "briefer" method for dispensing the Lord's Supper, resolved to implement "one sitting."[18] Clearly, by the opening decades of the 20th century, Cape Breton's sacramental season seemed cut adrift from its original moorings and found a great variety of expressions among many different congregations.

Some of the changes were not dictated by convenience, but by the inroads of the temperance and hygiene movements. The age of science and the advances of microbiological theory cast the traditional communion in a new light as a potential bearer of disease. Set against this background, the Lord's Supper became increasingly an expression of "holy hygiene" rather than the "worship of God": a ritual more concerned with microbes than grace.[19] In Cape Breton congregations, the conventional goblet was quickly retired and supplanted by the use of the so-called "wee cups," that is, individual cups.[20] The congregation of Margaree embraced this new practice in 1905 as did St Ann's in 1910. Port Morien church officials made the same decision in 1911 and decided to give one of its "old communion cups" to Mrs. A. McVicar as a souvenir in recognition of her "caring for them during the last number of years."[21] Grand River and Catalone fell into line with changed policy in 1915 and 1919 respectively.[22] In August, 1913, Sydney Mines boasted that they had used the "Peerless" individual communion service for the first time.[23] In some congregations, the rejection of the single goblet was greeted with dissension. There were those church members who dismissed the individual cups as a fad while others endorsed them on sanitary grounds. One exponent defended this innovation as more conducive to the female "sense of delicacy and refinement."[24] Although presented with an individual communion service in 1914, Boularderie waited for ten years to adopt the new system, finally acquiescing to the recommendations of the Department of Health and to the compelling arguments of a local elder who pointed out "that they had already begun to use two common cups and there could be no difference between two and two hundred seeing that they had departed from the use of one cup."[25] In 1899, the Session at Marion Bridge unanimously agreed to use unfermented wine for Communion.[26] The discontinuation of the traditions of using wine and a common cup were more than cosmetic. It fundamentally altered the old symbolic meanings of sitting around a long communion table gathered for a meal, serving one another "from hand to hand" and of pouring wine at the Lord's Table.[27] In short, it signified the precedence of the individual over community.[28]

Even the use of metal tokens was eventually abandoned, replaced by a system of printed cards. Port Morien effected this change in 1911, although congregations such as Boularderie postponed the adoption of paper tokens until the 1930s.[29]

Other aspects of the Presbyterian worship continued to stray from tradition. For example, organists and choirs increasingly supplanted Cape Breton's precentors. According to the Rev. John Murray, however, they refused to go down without a fight and managed to maintain their ascendancy into the early 20th century, "chiefly through the inherited conservatism and prejudice of ministers, sessions and older people" against choirs and musical instruments.[30] Many Cape Breton Presbyterian congregations battled over the merits of using the organ as a form of musical worship. The staunch defenders of the precenting tradition mounted a vociferous resistance to the introduction of "a kist o'whistles" into their churches.[31] Others embraced these changes in stages. At Marion Bridge, for example, the congregation approved the introduction of a choir in 1904, although the use of an organ was not permitted for another five years. In 1905, the Session at East Lake Ainslie Presbyterian Church yielded to the appeals of a delegation of three young men requesting acceptance of the gift of a pump organ from "the young people of the parish."[32] Framboise resisted this herald of modernization until 1915. It appears that the laity were far more sympathetic towards the precentor's pretensions than many clergy. One apologist was Dr. Hugh N. MacDonald of Whycocomagh, a Queen's University graduate in 1882, who railed against the new innovation of the choir when he wrote:

> Instead of the solemnity of the revered old Precentors, whose position was at the foot of the sacred pulpit, we have an organ, an organist so called and a bunch of bleached individuals partially covered as what well might be termed a second edition of Zulu garb; who gigglingly take their alloted place, on the platform, back of the minister.[33]

In the 1940s, the voice of Rev. A. W. R. MacKenzie, founder of St. Ann's Gaelic College, joined those who decried the receding strength of Cape Breton's precenting tradition. He hurled salvos against those "innovators" who lobbied for shortened, more regularized tunes for the Scottish psalms, accusing them of eviscerating Gaelic's "rich ministry" and undermining "the age-long, traditional mode and intonations of 'The Fathers.'"[34]

It is important to note that during the early 20th century, certain rural areas of Cape Breton stood firm against the trend to modernize, and struggled to preserve the traditional Sàcramaid. Framboise, for example, continued to celebrate its five-day outdoor communion; in September 1906, more than 1500 people assembled at the "Tent" for English and Gaelic services.[35] Loch Lomond, Grand River and West Bay perpetuated the custom until at least 1912. At Black River, the traditional open-air service also persisted. Here, in June 1915, after "some consideration" both English and Gaelic services were staged outdoors.[36] In 1919, communion tables were installed indoors; although in July 1920, it was agreed that services would be "in the open air" if the weather was "favorable." Boularderie hung on longer than most, until 1921.[37]

But these last strongholds were the exception, not the norm. The residual retention of this religious festival in rural Cape Breton into the 20th century barely disguised the fact that the outdoor Gaelic communion was a doomed tradition.

The decline of the open-air Sàcramaid was also reflected in the changed deportment of some of its participants. Admittedly, there were lapses in behaviour at the mid-19th century communions. In August 1853, for example, two young men, labelled as "worthless characters," "annoyed those around them" at the communion in Sydney Mines.[38] Their conduct was atypical, however, sharply contrasting with the decorum and reverence of the main body of worshippers. On the whole, public behaviour seems to have been pious and respectful. The Rev. A. Ross insisted in his memoirs: "I never knew anything of the kind which Robert Burns describes in his 'Holy Fair'."[39] Ross was probably whitewashing the situation. There were undoubtedly some restlessness, furtive glances, traded notes and whispered exchanges, especially among the younger participants, many of whom congregated "to see and meet their friends."[40] Needless to say, the misconduct of "careless youths"[41] could be quickly checked by the flashed glances from the vigilant elders who patrolled the grounds or by a verbal thunderbolt from one of the ministers like the one who stopped in the middle of his discourse to harangue: "When Sandy Cameron is dune wi'teeklin' Jean MacPherson, the service o'God will proceed."[42] There was no refuge from the gimlet-eyed stare of these implacable defenders of the faith.

By the 1870s, the open-air communion was losing some of its solemnity. American journalist, Charles Dudley Warner, author of *Baddeck, and that Sort of Thing*, claimed that the communion season had become marred by "days of license, of carousing, of drinking, and of other excesses."[43] He remarked that a tradition so sordidly debased required some drastic reformation. Although Warner had a journalistic propensity for anecdote and caricature, additional evidence gives weight to some of his allegations. For example, in September 1876, the *North Sydney Herald* railed against the "driving about, walking to and fro, laughing and swearing" at some of these gatherings. The *Herald* exclaimed: "It is high time that these out-door gatherings, relics of persecution days, were abandoned...."[44]

Such antics became more commonplace in the 1880s. According to American journalist, Charles Farnham, the communions were increasingly scandalized by young people flirting, exchanging notes, throwing motto candies—which bore such cheeky endearments as "You're the girl for me"—huddling at the back of the crowd, wandering among the horses and buggies and conversing in undertones.[45] He cited one instance when young men had stashed some firecrackers and a whisky bottle in a nearby wagon.

According to *The Blue Banner,* the "wife seeker" was the pariah of the open-air communions. He could be easily spotted with his oiled hair, white paper collar, patent leather boots, pockets full of conversation lozenges and an umbrella "ready to shelter the object of his adoration from either scorching sun rays or pelting rain."[46] There were other disreputable intruders like the Louisbourg tavern keeper who as bold as brass sold "heather dew" and "Jamaica punch" in the woods near the communion site at Mira.[47]

Another example clearly symptomatic of the decline of the Sàcramaid was the unwillingness of participants to endure the discomforts of the past. In July, 1889, the people attending Boularderie's open-air communion fled from the rain and sought shelter in a nearby church for the Gaelic service.[48] Further evidence of a tradition under assault is reflected in the changes in attire, for later accounts describing this event refer to parasols, sunshades, umbrellas or weatherproofs—comforts which to an earlier generation had connoted physical and spiritual effeteness. One late-19th-century account actually stipulated that a "green umbrella with a knobby handle, was absolutely necessary for such a solemn occasion, whether the elements warranted its use or not."[49] Photographs of outdoor sacramental gatherings from the same period also testify to the use of blankets at these later communions.

For young people, the communion season had lost much of its spiritual mystique. Nevertheless, the event retained its social function and served principally as a forum for courtship. In Will Pringle's words, the communion season pro-

83

vided a welcome chance "to meet a new girl and do some 'sparking'."[50] Most printed sources are silent about sexual improprieties at the open-air communions, but there is no doubt that innocent flirtations sometimes crossed the line.[51] The Rev. Angus McQueen, one-time moderator of the United Church of Canada, claims that some communion season romances were even consummated. He states plainly:"I am told that occasionally the emotional pitch and sociability got out of hand, and a number of babies were born nine months later."[52] Pringle's recollections are equally frank: "Oh boy! At some of these there were more souls made than saved!"[53] Alfred McKay of Militia Point, born around 1905, went to several open-air communions at Cleveland where the young people "camped out and carried on all night…. There were a lot of illegal [sic] children born after it."[54] Catherine Poole's version of the youthful mirth was a little more sanitized:"Young folks made the most of it. They had lots of fun." Of course, premarital sex and illegitimate offspring were taboo subjects in a society where people still talked about babies"coming in a satchel."[55]

Fig. 15 The open-air sacrament in 1885, from a drawing by A. B. Frost. From Harper's New Monthly Magazine 1885/1886 Reprinted with permission of Harper's Magazine.

The evolving dress code at open-air communions also betrayed relaxed standards. Homemade clothing was no longer so prevalent among the worshippers. In fact, as Charles Dunn observes in his book, *Highland Settler*, homespun, once a "respected symbol" of virtue, "was scorned by the rising generation as the symbol of outmoded poverty."[56] This change in communion-season attire even made its way into the more remote areas of settlement. The Rev. John Murray, who attended a communion at Cape North in July 1910, observed that the men in the congregation "dress as neatly and fashionably as anywhere else" while the women "wear more modern headgear and the girls wear hats of the latest style."[57] The communion became the place to flaunt fashionable finery, particularly for the young women who had returned home from the "Boston States" for a summer vacation. These visits were often timed to correspond with an open-air communion. At the communions in the 1880s, these women stood out conspicuously in their fancy bonnets and pin-back dresses—they

Fig. 16 Late 19th-century communion service at Mira, NS. Reprinted with permission of Union Presbyterian Church, Mira Ferry.

85

came from another place, from the world of the big city.[58] To many local residents, these displays were overly pretentious. "Anybody who came back home from Boston were way up in the world—or at least they thought they were ... even if they were there only for two weeks."[59] Francis MacGregor's *Days that I Remember* recalls with wry bemusement the "girls" who staged an appearance "minus their Cape Breton accents," but decked out in "their wide brimmed hats topped with a huge ostrich plume, and long silk skirts that made swishing sounds as they marched in triumph into the church."[60] Their arrival "would make heads turn and whispering would start." It is doubtful that piety was foremost in the minds of the couple described in *Pringle's Mountain*, who caught many eyes as they headed towards the Malagawatch communion in their hand-some black wagon with red-painted wheels and a glossy brown "high stepping morgan mare."[61] The older women refused to yield to fashion trends and clung to the tradition of the old bonnet.

Fig. 17 Cape Breton Presbyterians on *the way to the yearly sacrament, c. 1890.* From C. W. Vernon, Cape Breton at the Beginnings of the Twentieth Century. *Toronto: Nation Publishing, 1908.*

How-ever, for many Cape Breton women it now became accepted practice that "everything new made its appearance at the Sacrament time."[62] The sombre, monochromatic attire of worshippers of an earlier generation was now punctuated by variegated flashes of colour and finery. According to Dolly McKay, "Everybody had special clothes for it." Catherine Ross recalled that her mother's circle of friends frequently exchanged among themselves cloth flowers, bows or feathers to ornament their straw hats.

It is interesting to note that young children were more visible at the later communions. Catherine Ross recalled going to her first open-air communion at Little Narrows in 1906 when she was only four. She lay on the grass because the plank benches were so hard, and as the hours dragged on, she rested her head on her father's knee. When the service was over, he swept her up on his shoulders so she would not be trampled. Dolly McKay, whose family lived at Kempt Head, attended her first open-air communion at eight years of age on the hill above Knox Church, Boularderie. The experience filled her with wide-eyed amazement. "You never saw so many people." She "sat on the ground ... squirming and stretching her legs," her eyes drawn to the large plumed hats. "You couldn't be looking around at the hats or anything.... You'd get a nudge." Flora MacMillan of Catalone remembered attending an open-air communion at five or six years of age in 1915. She reminisced that she "was tired out sitting there ... and I was hungry. There didn't seem to be any end to it." Hunger finally got the better of her and she burst out: "When am I going to get bread?"[63] For Catherine Poole, it was the Ceist that proved a childhood ordeal, as she fidgeted and cast sidelong glances at "her mother's watch."

It is worth remembering that the forbearance of many children raised in the Presbyterian faith, with its Shorter Catechism drummed into them, was sorely tested by the stern discipline and stringencies that set their mark on generation after generation. Ninety-year-old Alfred Mckay, of Militia Point, recalled in 1995 with little fondness the rigours of family worship, especially the imposed silence during morning prayers, usually held around 6 a.m., while the porridge sat warming on the stove. John Morrison of Nyanza recounted in 1927 that the long family prayers were an endurance test for him during his childhood. He acted out his frustration by chewing the backs of the wooden chairs that the family had brought from Scotland.[64] One six-year-old from the Kempt Head area found her grandfather's heavy dose of prayer and Bible readings three times a day, morning, noontime and suppertime, too much to bear. As a childish prank born of desperation, she took a stick and wedged it into the barn door, trying to block his exit after his morning chores. "I'll fix you old man" she thought spitefully. She would have left him there indefinitely had it not been for her grandmother's interventions. Their following conversation highlights intergenerational religious tension:

> "Did you see Grandpa?"
> "Yes."
> "Where is he?"
> "I locked him in."
> "Very good dear, you locked him in. Was that nice?"
> "Well, that kept him from praying for awhile."
> "Let's go let him out. Now you tell your grandfather what you did."
> "I locked you in the barn."
> "Why did you do that dear?"
> "I was tired of your praying."[65]

All the changes in public behaviour at the open-air communions did not escape the attention of Cape Breton's Presbyterian clergy. They became increasingly disillusioned about the spiritual merits of the sacramental gatherings. Some ministers suspected that the expatriates on their summer visits had become a conduit for doctrinal havoc. "Errors are brought among us chiefly by men that return from the United States," asserted one Cape North minister.[66] Equally distressing was the fact that "fun" and revelry were crowding out spiritual edification.[67] One writer bemoaned in 1904 that the communions attracted "pleasure seekers, rowdies and town hoodlums."[68] These congested gatherings, which offered a host of temptations, had become "debased" by horsetrading, fraternizing and even tippling. According to the *MacTalla*, Mira's sacramental seasons "for a number of years" had been degraded by "a lot of misbehaviour and disorder ... due to the corrupt exchange of drink."[69] It was with some degree of horror that the Presbyterian Session at Grand River met in July 1884 to discuss rumours that liquor "was being sold at Communion time."[70] The litter of bottles near the communion sites left more conspicuous evidence of less spiritual, more spirituous preoccupations. One oral source recalled how her mother, assisted by curious offspring, salvaged the bottles, removed the necks and adapted them for preserves.[71]

No example better illustrates the decline of the open-air season in Cape Breton than the childhood memories related in Angus Hector MacLean's *God and the Devil at Seal Cove*. At one turn-of-the-century communion, he found himself as a young boy scrambling gleefully on his hands and knees "between the rows of people" harvesting "a bonanza" of motto candies, which had been tossed around by the "young swains."[72] This was not an isolated incident. At another open-air service, these notorious sugar candies were so prolific that they created a hail-like din as they careened off the sun parasols of worshippers.[73]

Evidently the open-air communion of the early-20th century bore little similarity to its early-19th-century predecessor. Undoubtedly, it was a casualty of a transformed Cape Breton. During the late 19th century, this region underwent far-reaching economic, cultural, demographic and technological changes. From the 1840s to 1890s, there was a myriad of important transitions: from log to frame house; from weekly to daily mail between Halifax and Cape Breton; from one Cape Breton colliery to more than fourteen in opera-tion; and from treacherous bridle paths to well-defined stage and railway routes.[74] By the 1880s, Sydney, even before its rapid industrialization at the turn of the century, took on the temperament and tempo of a major urban centre: ocean steamers, as well as schooners and fishing smacks, frequented its harbours; steamers plied daily between Sydney, North Sydney and Port Mulgrave; and morning newspapers from Halifax reached Sydney readers by evening. Equally significant were the demographic shifts as manifested in rural depopulation, internal migration and outmigration.[75] This phenomenon is documented in the Presbyterian communion rolls for this period. These registers offer sober commentary on the attrition of rural communicants with such telling phrases as "went to Boston" or "removed west."[76] All these changes were bound to have a significant impact on the character and traditions of the inhabitants of Cape Breton: in short, they bore directly on the whole process of cultural transmission.

During this period, the Presbyterian church underwent its own metamorphosis, especially in terms of structural and professional expansion. In the 1840s, the Presbytery of Sydney (which included Cape Breton County and portions of Victoria and Richmond Counties) comprised two ordained ministers, two organized congregations, approximately eight elders and ninety communicants. By the 1880s, the Presbytery boasted thirteen ministers and congregations, 100 elders and 1200 communicants.[77] Clearly, by the late 19th century, there were strong forces reshaping Cape Breton, and the crest of change carried the Communion Season tradition in a new direction.

The clergymen themselves played a role in its trans-formation. Throughout the closing decades of the 19th century, Presbyterian clergy increasingly stigmatized the open-air communion as an old-fashioned contradiction of the "fashions of the living age."[78] Their aversion to this established custom was much more complex than a simple distaste for an anachronism. In the late 1870s, there was a movement afoot to regulate the open-air communions. In August 1878, for example, several members attending a meeting of the Presbytery of Richmond and Victoria tabled a resolution condemning "large gatherings of people on Sacramental occasions."[79] Their more senior co-presbyters were hesitant to tamper with a tradition "which prevailed in all parts of Scotland and in all branches of the Church."[80] Moreover, this matter, they argued, fell within the jurisdiction of the Kirk Sessions. The issue proved contentious enough to command the attention of the Synod of the Maritime Provinces several months later. There, the Rev. Alexander F. Thompson of Mabou, teamed with the Rev. John Maclean of Broad Cove, particularized on the "evils" and "abuses." In their minds, the sacramental gatherings should be reviled not glorified: "In days gone by these meetings were no doubt very useful, but their usefulness has ceased." The Rev. Murdoch Stewart of Whycocomagh, backed by fellow apologist Rev. Kenneth MacKenzie of Baddeck, took the defensive, claiming that reported abuses were "extremely exaggerated." In fact, Stewart asserted that during his thirty-two-year tenure in Cape Breton, he had no first-hand knowledge of these alleged irregularities. He conceded that the time-honoured tradition was flawed, but insisted "there are also great benefits."[81]

This conflict highlighted an interesting breach, for it pitted Stewart and MacKenzie, two veteran Gaelic-speaking preachers, against Thompson and Maclean, two young and recently-ordained ministers; it is doubtful that the latter were fluent Gaelic speakers. The dichotomy starkly revealed that a new generation of clergy in Cape Breton had less appreciation for the open-air communion. They did not regard themselves as conservators of tradition, but as agents of reform.

Throughout the 1880s, the injunction "Let all things be done decently and in order"became the popular axiom among Cape Breton's Presbyterian clergy.[82] In 1889, more drastic measures were taken against the open-air communions when the Victoria and Richmond Presbytery stipulated that henceforth"so far as practicable, the communions be held in contiguous congregations on the same Sabbath."[83] This decision marked a sharp break from the past, when communions were scheduled expressly to avoid conflict with those in other congregations. The Rev. John Rose applauded this new rule, writing on November 5, 1889: "on no occasion since his pastorate were the services connected with the communion more orderly and satisfactory."[84] The policy of simultaneous communions in adjacent parishes effectively curtailed the size and population base of sacramental gatherings. Some clergy assigned other salutary effects, rationalizing, for example, that the absence of swarming crowds facilitated proper mental preparation for the Lord's Supper. Participants, they argued, were now spared the distractions of added "home cares"which had formerly impeded meditation and"quiet of mind."[85] Interestingly enough, there is no record of any public resistance to these changes.

Even in its abbreviated form, the open-air communion elicited criticism from its detractors. One *Presbyterian Witness* correspondent observed in August 1897: "some of our ministers are of opinion that part of the attendance might well be dispensed with, as a number are drawn by the desire of seeing friends … and some by even less worthy motives."[86] The next logical step was to bring the service indoors, into a more controlled and ordered setting. The adoption of the indoor communion dramatically reshaped the meaning of this sacrament for many Cape Breton Presbyterians. Whereas the open-air communion emphasized lay fellowship, historic continuity and communal life, the indoor communion would give symbolic prominence to approved doctrine and ministerial authority.[87]

Clerical intervention also transformed the Ceist, as ministers increasingly inserted themselves into this so-called "people's own democracy festival."[88] Although "speaking to the question" was traditionally the privilege of "the Men," an account of Cape North's 1874 communion season indicates that several ministers, as well as three laymen, spoke at this event. At a Ceist at Big Island (Boularderie) in September 1905, three of the discussants were clerics.[89] The spontaneity of the Friday discourse was further checked by the growing tendency of the Clerk of Session to "select a question" in advance for the Friday service.[90] In August 1917, at River Denys, the question was announced several weeks before the Ceist. There was certainly no decline in the number of participants at some of the early 20th-century Cape Breton Ceists. In 1905, at Indian Brook, Victoria County, twenty-one "spoke to the question"; fifteen held the floor at Grand River in August 1915.[91] But quantity was not synonymous with quality. In fact, there is some evidence that the calibre of the Ceist performances was slipping and that the new generation of "the Men" had less force and spirit than their predecessors. In 1913, the *Presbyterian Witness* reported that participants at the Ceist "are not now the outstanding men of olden days in Highland congregations."[92] Some of the Friday speakers inspired more annoyance than awe, more ridicule than reverence. And although their Ceist-day performances were far from edifying, a "lot of the old fellows thought they could talk better than the minister."[93] Dolly McKay recalled "one old feller getting up [who] had no sense to quit" and expostulated for a "terrible long time." Whitman Gillis's impressions were similar: "A lot spoke there who shouldn't have." Catherine Ross remembered her bemusement over "one old fellow" who frequently got "overheated" and "worked up" and earned the local nickname "Billy Friday" after the flamboyant American pulpit thumper, "Billy Sunday." John MacLeod of Big Bras D'Or (known locally as "John Bliss"), an eloquent Ceist speaker, was somewhat disdainful of his second-rate colleagues. At one Friday prayer meeting, he held back and declined an invitation to participate with this retort, which was no less than a slur on their competence: "When the chickens are through scratching, there's not much for the hen to do."[94] Among a new generation of young Cape Bretoners, the Ceist day lost its spiritual aura and was called disparagingly "the old Man's Day."[95] In rural Cape Breton, it hung on, but only as a relic of the past. In Black River, for example, the Presbyterian Church held Ceists until the late 1930s. However, attendance at these events was woefully small. In 1937, the Session minutes referred to "few people" at the Friday gathering; the following year, the same refrain was echoed: "Few were present at the service."[96]

The most devastating blow to "the Men's" influence was the Maritime Synod's decision to replace the traditional Gaelic lay catechist with a probationer, that is, a divinity student. This development had drastic repercussions for "the Men," many of whom had honed their preaching talents and consolidated their influence as catechists. Its ultimate impact was to curtail the participatory aspects of the communion season, to dethrone "the Men" as a force at the Sàcramaid and relegate them to a minor role.[97] Although retained in many turn-of-the-century rural Gaelic-speaking congregations, the once "glorious" Ceist day also began to fade with the deaths of such saintly men as Malcolm MacLeod and Donald Ross, both in 1877, Angus McLeod in 1878, Donald MacAulay in 1886, Angus McLean in 1892, Donald MacDonald in 1897 and Donald Campbell in 1900.[98] For the Rev. John Murray there was more than a tenuous link between the demise of the open-air communion in Cape Breton and the decline of these "venerable patriarchs." "Our open air communions in Cape Breton," he stated categorically, "began to lose their interest to our people, when the prayerful, humble, holy and spirit-taught men who came from Scotland in the early part of the last century, began to pass away."[99] Sentimentalism, notwithstanding, Murray failed to acknowledge the fact that church policy had effectively thwarted the emergence of a new generation of "Men" to carry the torch of tradition.

Why did certain Cape Breton clergy in the late 19th century become so antagonistic towards the open-air communion?
Why were they so eager to rein in and ultimately suppress
this tradition? In part, their antipathy mirrored the ascent of
industrial capitalism and its new cultural interpretation of
time.[100] The five-day annual religious festival, rooted in the
seasonal rhythms of pre-industrial times, was increasingly
anomalous in a world governed by clocks and convenience,
work schedules and economic output. Moreover, the spate
of church building throughout late 19th-century Canada reflected the growing popularity of the architectonic ideals that
proclaimed faith through built space. These initiatives also
gave material expression to the growing desire of Canada's
mainstream Protestant and Catholic churches to achieve
a more "tactile witness of spiritual devotion" and to display
prosperity and permanence.[101] According to Vicki Bennett,
author of *Sacred Space and Structural Style*, as these aspira-
tions waxed, "the romantic image of the simple but rugged
preacher praying in the fields to the gathered multitude of
simple folk began to fade from popularity."[102] Is it therefore
possible that the patina of nostalgia in Cape Breton for the
leafy "temples" of worship in its glens and glades wore thin
for the same reasons?[103]

Evidence also indicates that by the late 19th century,
many clergymen also recoiled from the emotional physicality
and spontaneity of earlier outdoor communions.[104] Whereas
earlier clergy such as the Rev. Hugh McLeod regarded religiosity as the barometer of success at an open-air sacramental
gathering, late-19th-century clergy became shameless apolo-
gists for the bourgeois virtue of respectability, reviling un-
bridled fervour and priding themselves on maintaining order,
reason and restraint. These became the new watchwords for
Cape Breton's so-called "solemn season."[105] In July 1884, the
Rev. Donald MacDougall of West Bay boasted that there was
"no wild excitement in our meetings."[106] The accounts of later
communions published in the *MacTalla* reflected the growing
popularity of this new ideal. Of the Framboise communion in
August 1894, it was recorded: "We were very pleased to see
the pilgrims, and especially because they were so polite, so

orderly, and so sober."[107] The Little Narrows communion in July, 1894, was described thus: "Although there was a large crowd gathered they were all on their knees politely and staidly, and there wasn't any misbehaviour seen the whole day."[108] The communion service at Sydney, in August 1896, elicited the following comment: "The crowd was beautifully staid, and everything was done with elegance and in true order."[109] The Framboise sacramental ceremonies again merited praise in August, 1889: "Many were gathered at the time from the surrounding congregations and they were praised for how orderly and sober they were and that they stayed to the end of the service."[110]

Order and sobriety were the moral imperatives of a new generation of Cape Breton clergymen who formed the front ranks of the temperance movement.[111] As a group they condemned the more recreational aspects of religion and the traditional conjunction of solemnity and festivity. The sacramental season was only one of their targets in a far-reaching moralistic crusade which reached into both workplaces and holy places. In October, 1885, for example, the Presbytery of Sydney rallied against the increasing popularity of tea meetings, picnics and bazaars as fundraisers for churches. Such activities, it protested, promoted "dancing and frolicking."[112] To stamp out such unseemly levity, the Presbytery decreed that all fund-raising festivals connected with the church required both the consent and supervision of the Kirk Sessions and that dancing or "any other sinful practices" would not be tolerated at such meetings.[113]

In September, 1901, the Presbytery of Inverness declared war against mixed dancing, drunkenness and brawling at all summer gatherings.[114] In 1913, the Session of River Denys discountenanced church members participating in "dancing parties" and threatened to strike their names from the church roll.[115] In February, 1915, the Orangedale Session singled out dancing and card parties as leading social evils. Session officials were particularly distressed that some church members had "since our last Communion time promoted, participated and associated in these amusements." Had these privileged members in "full communion" not betrayed "their obligations and promises when received into church fellowship?" The Session agreed and held the threat of forfeiture of privileges over the heads of delinquent members "unless they appear before the Session, and give reason why this ought not to be done."[116] In 1913, the Session at Marion Bridge also frowned on Christian jollity and introduced its own austere measures which were aimed directly at the choir members. They passed the following resolution: "Whereas dancing by members of the choir has been a source of trouble in the past in this congregation; therefore resolved to have none in the choir but those who will abstain from the questionable habit of dancing."[117] In channelling their congregations toward moderation and conformity, Cape Breton's Presbyterian clergy were hardly a small isolated band of moralistic reformers. They were standard-bearers in a larger international movement toward regulating popular behaviour and "gentrifying" public celebrations.[118]

The demise of the open-air communion in Cape Breton can also be linked to the decline of Gaelic. Throughout the

Fig. 18 Centennial sacrament at Baddeck, NS, near the site of original Knox Church on Baddeck Bay Road, 10 August 1941. Reprinted with permission of Mrs. Muriel Kaiser.

19th century, there was a lamentable shortage of Gaelic-speaking clergy in Cape Breton. Periodically, there were poignant appeals to redress this shortcoming.[119] Judging from some of the discussions at Synod meetings, one suspects that such requests did not enjoy a sympathetic hearing.[120] For example, in 1858, the Rev. George Sutherland, a native of New Glasgow, denounced the continued prominence of the Gaelic language in certain Maritime Presbyterian congregations. He deemed this practice anachronistic alongside the supremacy of English as the language of law, literature and commerce. The continued use of Gaelic in the Presbyterian Church, he argued, impeded "the increase of the Church by throwing obstacles in the way of English settlers joining it" and prejudiced Gaelic-speaking people against "English ministers equally gifted and gracious with any that speak the Gaelic."[121] Sutherland urged the church to adopt a policy of assimilation:

> ...that whenever all the Church members of a congregation understood English to the extent of ordinary conversation, public worship should be conducted only in the language; and when one-fourth of the members understood no English they should receive just one-fourth of the services and so on in proportion.[122]

The Synod, it should be noted, did not adopt Sutherland's recommendations. But its membership clearly sympathized with his sentiments, as indicated by an account of the debate in the *Presbyterian Witness*:

> ...all felt and owned the importance of promoting the study of English and of English literature, since it is the language of our country and since a want of due familiarity with it would stand seriously in the way of the material and spiritual progress of the people.[123]

This statement was nothing less than an assertion of linguistic chauvinism by church officials who failed to appreciate that among Gaelic-speakers this "language of the Garden of Eden" enjoyed a special cachet as the idiom of religion.

Gaelic-speaking Cape Bretoners, discouraged by the inaction of the Synod in recruiting fluent clergy, looked hopefully to their own home-grown ministers to fill the vacuum. But here again, they were disappointed as their young men returned from the theological college in Halifax, proficient in Greek and Hebrew with their Gaelic rusty from disuse.[124] Other changes were manifested as well among the new generation of theology graduates who turned their backs on the distinctive conventions of Gaelic preaching and embraced a more intellectual approach which emphasized the use of a prepared text and more cosmopolitan tone.

The Presbyterian Church in Cape Breton was hardly an active agent in stemming Gaelic's decline. In fact, its role was somewhat ambiguous, given the fact that religious services during the 19th century, even in Gaelic-speaking strongholds, had a bilingual format.[125] For example, although the communicants at Cape North's sacramental season in 1874 were uniformly Gaelic-speaking (there was not even an English "table"), an "action" sermon was preached in English all the same.[126] Twenty years later, even in this Gaelic stronghold, the signs of linguistic assimilation were visible. One correspondent to the *MacTalla* harangued:"They leave the house of worship as soon as the English service is over as if they didn't have a word of Gaelic in their heads."[127]

Cape Breton's Gaelic speakers had little choice but to turn to the hoary-headed old guard to meet their linguistic needs rather than the freshly-minted clerics from the Presbyterian College in Halifax. As late as 1904, the seventy-six-year-old Rev. David Drummond, of Big Bras d'Or, was still an important fixture at local communions, even though he was well past his clerical prime. His fluency in Gaelic, although a much-depreciated asset among a growing number of Cape Breton Presbyterians, still attracted a loyal following. *The Blue Banner* of October, 1904, singled Drummond out for special mention:"Father Drummond is considered an indispensable of a really successful Summer Sacrament season in this and that of the Gaelic congregations of our Island."[128]

In 1907, an outspoken lobby of Gaelic-speaking activists in Nova Scotia tried to mobilize both pulpit and press to convince members of the Presbyterian Church of the worthiness of inaugurating a Gaelic lectureship at the Presbyterian College in

Halifax. In the front ranks of this cause were two native-born Cape Bretoners, Hon. William Ross, one-time storeowner and postmaster at Englishtown, a Liberal politician and senator, and the Rev. Murdoch A. MacKinnon, a minister at the Park Street Church, Halifax, and a member of the celebrated Lake Ainslie MacKinnon family that produced no fewer than five ministers.[129] Along with the Rev. S. D. McPhee of Belfast, Prince Edward Island, they highlighted the deplorable shortage of Gaelic-speaking ministers in Maritime Canada and the extensive number of vacancies in Gaelic-speaking congregations. For almost one year, the columns of the *Presbyterian Witness* hosted a tense debate about the merits of promoting the use of Gaelic among young candidates for the ministry. One correspondent, dubbing himself *Eileanach*, touched a raw nerve with his rejoinder that the cause was more "inglorious" than noble and was bound to fail.[130] He noted that the double preaching services required in Gaelic congregations, as well as the limited career prospects for Gaelic-speaking clergy, were an insurmountable deterrent which rendered the notion of a Gaelic lectureship both "sentimental" and "extravagant."[131] He accused the activists of "bleeding" Gaelic-speaking Presbyterians to subsidize what would be little more than a "sinecure."[132] *Eileanach*'s most provocative salvo was his comment that "Possibly too much Gaelic preaching has kept Highlanders so [poor and unprogressive]. Hyper-Calvinism in Gaelic is a paralyzing essence, and has had deplorable results on both sides of our seas."[133]

Another Cape Bretoner, J. A. McLellan, who was ordained and inducted as a minister in St. Ann's-Englishtown in 1908, also joined the fray. By comparison, his remarks were more temperate. He conceded that there were no less than four "vacant fields" in Cape Breton requiring Gaelic catechists; he did not, however, endorse the plans for a Gaelic chair.[134] "I will venture to prophesy," he concluded dolefully, "that if Gaelic-speaking parents continue, as they now do, in failing to teach their children Gaelic, in twenty years there will be very little or no Gaelic demand to be supplied even in St. Ann's."[135] Such slights unleashed a fury of wounded Highland pride. Hon. William Ross and Dr. John Cameron of Port Hood launched a blistering counterattack and invoked the memory of a host of celebrated Gaels to defend the honour of their fellow Highlanders.[136] The editor of the *Presbyterian Witness* noted with bemusement:"One thing these letters have shown is that whether the Gaelic language be dying or not, the Highland spirit is very much alive."[137]

Ultimately, the campaign for a Gaelic lectureship at the Presbyterian College in Halifax bore little fruit. Ross, MacKinnon and their fellow supporters in the Scottish Gaelic community had to be content with the fact that Dalhousie and St. Francis Xavier Universities engaged the services of the Rev. Alexander Maclean Sinclair as a Gaelic lecturer. They exhorted students at the Presbyterian College to avail themselves of his classes in Gaelic language and literature and Celtic Civilization in order to hone their preaching skills in the"dear 'mother tongue'."[138] This slim victory, however, rang hollow. Ross was embittered by the fact that so few of the clergy, to whom he had personally appealed for donations to subsidize a Gaelic lectureship, were willing to dig into their pockets. He wrote:"Of the clergymen to whom we have written, four had the courtesy to respond and will remit the sum mentioned. The others have remained silent without even acknowledging the receipt of our letter. Perhaps they are so busy with Church work or so indifferent that they do not care whether the language in which they preach every Sunday is continued by their congregation...."[139] Ross even nursed some lingering resentment that the majority of the Synod members from Maritime Canada had voted against the proposal to rename The Presbyterian College in Halifax after St. Columba, the celebrated Scottish divine.[140] Clearly, the Presbyterian Church in Nova Scotia could not be depended upon to champion the use of the Gaelic language in the pulpit and to help reclaim its departed greatness.

On his visit to Cape Breton in 1932, John Campbell witnessed first-hand the erosion of the Scottish language culture in even the most staunchly Gaelic-speaking districts of eastern Nova Scotia. He concluded that Gaelic's prospect of survival was bleak. His notations read like an obituary:

Ingonish an English settlement.
Cape North—still Gaelic.
Bay of St. Lawrence—Catholic.
Lake Ainslie and Strathlorne. Minister A. S. MacLean, who
has no Gaelic. Not preached-United Church, and losing
ground.
Grand Mira. Gaelic strong, but little Gaelic preached.
Fourchu. Scots and French.
Port Hastings. A little Gaelic (Dr. D. MacDonald).
Hawkesbury. None (Protestants) but RCs, yes.
Margaree. English.
Margaree Forks. Gaelic.
Mabou, Glendale, Judique. Catholics use Gaelic.
Loch Lomond, St. Peter's, Grand River. No
preaching—Gaelic.
Gabarus?
Inverness. Gaelic not preached.
River Dennis, Gaelic 1911-20 when he himself was there
(Rev. J. A. MacLellan) no Gaelic since. Only occasionally
used in church.
Orangedale. Only occasionally used.
Little Narrows. do.
West Bay. Strong years ago, now dead.
Boularderie. Gaelic strong.
Louisbourg—mixed.
Iona—R.C.[141]

Campbell stopped short of pointing the finger of blame at any
particular culprit for this sorry state of affairs, but he did note
parethentically that Church Union and the emergence of the
United Church were far from being innocent bystanders. He
recounted that he was told "many times" in 1932 and 1937 that
Church Union had been "a severe setback to Gaelic."[142] A. W.
R. MacKenzie was less veiled in his assessment of the situation. In the early 1940s, he identified the declining fortunes
of Cape Breton's precentors as one of the central catalysts
in Gaelic's decline, stating bluntly that the precentor had
contributed "more than any other, to the preservation of the
Gaelic language in Rural Cape Breton ... [and] that in the
Gaelic community where the Precentor has ceased to function that, there Gaelic is on the decline."[143]

The underlying causes of the erosion of the Gaelic language among the younger population in Cape Breton are much-debated topics.[144] For most of the 19th century, Cape Breton's Gaelic-speaking culture had been protected by a carapace of shared religious affiliations, in-group marriages and relative isolation. However, the thick weave of kith and kin began to unravel as rural youth sought enlarged economic opportunities outside their own communities during the late 19th century.[145] The erosion of Cape Breton's rural base, along with the twin forces of urbanization and industrialization, dealt a devastating blow to the deeply rooted sense of Gaelic identity. In his monograph, *Gaelic Nova Scotia: An Economic, Cultural and Social Impact Study*, Michael Kennedy examines the causal connections among these related phenomena. He states plainly: "rural decline in eastern Nova Scotia was Gaelic decline."[146] Those people who streamed into the coal mining towns were exposed to ethnically, religiously and linguistically plural environments, often devoid of institutional structures which had once buttressed Gaelic's survival. Like an outgoing tide, Gaelic retreated "from the public to the private domain" and children were increasingly socialized in predominantly anglicized environments.[147] As many of the shared cultural reference points were swept away, "ethnicity became less a way of life than a symbolic attachment."[148] The loss of Gaelic, however gradual, weakened the link between religion and ethnicity, and further accentuated the irrelevance of the open-air communion, especially among young people, in the early 20th century.

The demise of the open-air communion was lamentable. In the lives of Presbyterian Cape Bretoners, this tradition had fulfilled several important functions. In one sense, it was a utilitarian response to the harsh economic realities of early 19th-century Cape Breton. For example, when Rev. Alexander Farquharson visited Loch Lomond, in 1833, there was no church. He preached instead in the open field, resting his Bible on a rough stump; it became known in local circles as the "Stump Pulpit." By 1846, there were only five Free Church ministers on the whole island, working among the diffusely settled Presbyterians. Some communities like Mira, Catalone,

Cow Bay, Grand River, Sydney, Gabarus, River Inhabitants, Strait of Canso and Baddeck lacked regular ministrations until 1850. Their contact with religion was tenuous. Only the yearly celebration of the Lord's Supper gave them a chance to share a deep religious experience, reducing the effects of spiritual destitution and spatial isolation. Even as late as the 1860s, many Presbyterian churches were small and unfinished, completely inadequate to the demands of large-scale gatherings.[149] Consequently, well into the 1880s, the open-air communion mitigated the isolation imposed by geography, demographic dispersion and poor communications. It signalled a victory over physical seclusion, deprivation and separation. As in Scotland, this cultural practice, which started as an expression of expediency and necessity, over time became an honoured expression of custom.

These "ceremonial loci" were also, in both the literal and figurative senses, family reunions.[150] By prescribing behaviour to a certain extent and by re-enacting rituals from a shared cultural past, participants at Cape Breton's 19th-century open-air communions gave symbolic expression to core communal values, and basic kin and religious loyalties. Although primarily a mixture of prayer and religious and kinship feasting, this open-air tradition was also an important venue for matchmaking. Margaret McPhail states in her novel, *Loch Bras d'Or*, "many weddings took place after these gatherings."[151] These "in-group" or endogamous marriages helped further to preserve group identity and a sense of cultural belonging. In sum, they were a vital ritual for "cultural maintenance."[152]

Although the Sàcramaid had communal power, the participants did not meld into a single homogeneous mass. After all, even though the entire community attended, very few people actually took communion. This event, in fact, helped highlight and validate boundary lines within the group.[153] The most conspicuous were the clearly drawn divisions between men and women, young, old and middle-aged, adherents and communicants, grace and non-grace. These differences were brought into focus and given ritual expression. Equally significant was the institutionalized distinction between English- and Gaelic-speakers. In this latter sense, the open-air communion encapsulated a "kin-religious-cultural as-semblage."[154] It was an overt expression of both a community and a Scottish highland ethnicity; by linking religion to ethnic heritage, this tradition doubly reinforced the participants' sense of identity.

The historic associations of the open-air communion also cemented ties to Scotland. For many Presbyterian immigrants, this recreation of Highland culture was a common thread from their immediate past. However, the sense of historic descent and continuous community generated by this event stretched back even further than that. Many devout Presbyterians re-garded these open-air communions as condensed re-enact-ments of the drama of the persecuted Covenanters who had sought out the safety of secluded glens for their forbidden worship under the "dome of the 'Cathedral of Immensity'."[155] The Scottish immigrants, who came to Cape Breton with their own story of persecution and expulsion felt a special identification with the Covenanters and, hence, the open-air communion, as a form of historical remembrance, celebrated renewed links between their present and their distant past.[156]

Food and the rites of hospitality also played an integral role within the framework of these open-air communions. In all societies, food and food sharing, both on a physical and spiritual plane, have pervasive symbolic significance. It is "one of the highest and most intimate forms of fellowship."[157] During Cape Breton's communion season, the sharing of food reinforced kinship interaction, further emphasizing subthemes of family and fellowship inherent in the ritual and theology of the Lord's Supper. Food was also the main com-ponent in a system of "ordered obligations," which balanced debts and favours, hospitality given and hospitality received.[158] Implicit in the tradition of communion season hospitality was the principle of reciprocal exchange which also served as connecting tissue. In short, it assured community interaction, reinforced group membership and strengthened the bonds of mutuality.

The communion season was also a faith-enhancing event. These "times of refreshing" were often scenes of "great ex-periences," sometimes marking the "beginning" or "climax" of a spiritual awakening.[159] And while these "experiences" were intensely personal, they were performed in a context that was vibrantly communal. During the mid-19th century, Presbyterian clergy in Cape Breton faithfully catalogued the telling signs of heightened piety demonstrated in the aftermath of the annual sacramental gatherings: "deep concern for the salvation of the soul,""remorse for sin,""brokenness of heart and spirit,""love to another,""family worship where formerly neglected," "meetings for prayers," "intense thirsting after the ordinances of religion" and "a visible outward amendment in life and conversion."[160] Cape Breton's open-air communions of 1870 and 1871 were particularly potent:"I may say in one word that there never was, in this country, such a season," wrote one *Presbyterian Witness* correspondent about Mira's communion in 1871.[161] The Rev. Hugh McLeod credited many salutary side-effects to this communion, including a remarkable proliferation of prayer meetings. By February 1872, he claimed that, within his congregation of Mira and Sydney, there were upwards of forty prayer meetings every week.[162] He even discerned an inward and outward reformation that was almost millennial in its perfection and social harmony. His parishioners were now "better husbands and better wives, better parents and better children, better masters and better servants, both friends and neighbours."[163] Not only did many mid-19th-century Presbyterian clergy value the spiritual benefits of open-air communions, but judging from the diary of William Jardine many laypersons cherished these events for the same reasons. One entry reads:

> Boularderie communion today where many shall sit down. Where many I trust shall taste the Lord is gracious, and unto whose hearts the light of God's reconciled countenance shall be made to shine….[164]

According to American historian, Leigh Schmidt, the richly nuanced religious symbolism of the open-air communion should not be discounted. Essentially, the mingling of "sermons and psalms, careful gestures and frenetic ones, long tables and consecrated elements, tokens and tears, thronged assemblies … prayers secret and public, conversions and diversions, visions and meditations" turned the extended sacramental gathering into "an awesome, powerful and transformative spectacle."[165] These components represented in a condensed way the panorama of Christian life and the human pilgrimage from penitence to thanksgiving, and from humiliation to joy.[166]

Into the 1920s, the "good old Highland custom" persisted in Cape Breton but only in those rural Gaelic-speaking areas where the "old order" prevailed.[167] By then, this annual event was increasingly viewed as an assembly of "old women" and "old grey-headed men," "dear old faces, weather-beaten with the storms of three-quarters of a century."[168] That basic perception was the reality, for the "old men and women," especially those who retained their Gaelic, figured most prominently at open-air communions by 1900. To all intents and purposes, Cape Breton's open-air communion had ceased to be a meaningful, culturally-shared tradition several decades earlier. It suffered a slow death as it was reformed into extinction. This landmark, which had at one time cemented friendships, strengthened faith and fostered a "strong class" of believers, became fragmented in its form and no longer generated consensus.[169] It became an event, where old people acted out historic rituals, young women came "busked in all their modest finery" and young men often cavorted.[170] As such, it made visible a social, cultural and moral conflict between the young and the old. It also made visible a tradition dismantled by the clergy, eroded by loss of heritage and reshaped by changed sensibilities and new values and imperatives.[171] In the larger sense, these changes reflected the decline of collective identity, shared meanings and world views among Cape Breton's Presbyterians. Even in its much diluted form, the Sàcramaid served as an expressive mirror of its times, revealing in its later years a much more complex and divisive society.

By the 1920s, Cape Breton Presbyterians increasingly travelled to the ever-diminishing number of communion sites by car. The traditional pilgrimage on foot was replaced by this 20th-century icon of individualism and material status. Jello became the dessert mainstay of the 20th-century communion season in Cape Breton. Some communion goers like Dolly

MacKay came to despise this culinary cliché. Hospitality now came in a prepackaged generic form and food preparation became synonymous with convenience and economy. A high degree of spiritual fellowship was also lost with the shift from the table to the pew. Communicants now took communion as "segregated households" sitting "in relative isolation from one another."[172]

The conjuncture of science and middle class values helped change both the form and the purpose of the Lord's Supper. Gone were the meanings of the common cup, the face-to-face posture and the corporate nature of worship. Much was lost and, some would say, little was gained with these changes. Ironically enough, in the more urbanized areas, Presbyterian clergy would find themselves bemoaning the extinction of the "fast day" and the decline in lay involvement as they strove to inject the "spirit of their old time outdoor sacraments" into the indoor communions.[173] But their noble lamentations were futile. The curtain had completely fallen on Cape Breton's once hallowed open-air communion tradition. The special beauty and impressiveness of this sacramental gathering could never be recaptured and would retreat into the shadows of human memory.

> The young folks who speak now the tongue of the Gael
> Wear ready made clothing from head to their feet;
> There's silk to their knees and tobacco to chew,
> With false teeth the stores sell they will chew up their food.
>
> They're coming each summer to South Haven here,
> There is nothing on earth that can keep them away;
> They've music and dancing with feasting and drink,
> But still give high honour to Norman MacLeod.
>
> We're not now as pious as the old folks of yore;
> Walking miles to the sermons so long:
> Their treasure was stored in the kingdom to come,
> It's only life's dust that's left us so blind.

So let us go now, my worthy dear friends.
To worship the one who's forgiven us all;
With Gaelic verses we'll be singing the praise
Of the people who conquered the hills and the vales.[174]

Notes to Chapter One

1. Private papers, Mrs. Emma McKay, Florence, "Spiritual Diary of William Jardine," entry for 1 August 1858.

2. *Presbyterian Witness* [henceforth *PW*], 15 January 1848.

3. Ibid., 14 September 1889.

4. Ibid., 15 January 1848.

5. Neville, *Kinship and Pilgrimage: Rituals of Reunion in American Protestant Culture*, 131.

6. *PW*, 21 September 1907; Cairns et al., The Holy Communion: A Symposium, 67-84.

7. Mullan's book, *Scottish Puritanism*, 1590-1638, provides a thoughtful analysis of the pervasive ambiguity inherent in Scottish Puritan thought about the nature and administration of communion. For a more detailed account of the communion tradition in Scotland, see Burnet, *The Holy Communion in the Reformed Church of Scotland, 1560-1960*; Schmidt, *Holy Fairs: Scottish Communions and American Revivals in the Early Modern Period*; Hunter, *The Making of the Crofting Community*; Hunter, "The Celebration of Communion in Scotland since the Reformation," *Records of the Scottish Church History Society*, 161-73; Ramsay and Koedel, "The Communion Season—An 18th Century Model," *Journal of Presbyterian History*, 203-16; Meek, "Evangelicalism and emigration: Aspects of the role of dissenting evangelicalism in Highland Emigration to Canada," in *Proceedings of the First North American Congress of Celtic Studies*, 15-25; Clarke "'Days of Heaven on Earth': Presbyterian Communion Seasons in Nineteenth-Century Otago," *Journal of Religious History*, 274-97; Owen, "The 'Communion Season' and Presbyterians in a Hebridean Community," *Gwerin*, 53-66; Parman, "Orduighean: A Dominant Symbol in the Free Church of the Scottish Highlands," *American Anthropologist*, 295-305.

8. Schmidt, *Holy Fairs, Scotland and the Making of American Revivalism* (2nd ed.), 15.

9. Ibid., 24.

10. Ibid., 33.

11. Ibid., 40.

12. Burns, *Old Scottish Communion Plate*, 2.

13. Ibid., 11.

14. MacDermid, *The Religious and Ecclesiastical Life of the Northwest Highlands*, 1750-1843, 194-95.

15. Burns, 112.

16. Ibid., xii.

17. The term "Kirk" can be used interchangeably with "Church of Scotland" which is the established national church in Scotland. The Presbyterian Church has a distinctive polity based on a hierarchy of courts composed of clerical and lay elders. They are, in ascending order, the Session, Presbytery, Synod and General Assembly. Each congregation is administered by its own Session presided over by the elders and minister. It is charged with responsibility for such matters as admission of new members, exercise of church discipline and arrangements for the administration of the sacraments.

18. Burns, 15

19. Ibid.

20. Ibid., 93, 113.

21. Quoted in MacDermid, 196.

22. Burns, 114.

23. MacInnes, *The Evangelical Movement in the Highlands of Scotland, 1688 to 1800*, 157. See also Smout, "Born Again at Cambuslang: New Evidence on Popular Religion and Literacy in Eighteenth-Century Scotland," *Past and Present*, 114-27 and Smith, "Distinguishing Marks of the Spirit of God: Eighteenth-Century Revivals in Scotland and New England."

24. Edgar, *Old Church Life in Scotland*, 179.

25. Burns, 115.

26. Burns, "The Holy Fair." The term houghmagandie was synonymous with immorality.

27. Drummond and Bulloch, *The Church in Victorian Scotland, 1843-1874*, 184.

28. Ibid.

29. MacDermid, 284.

30. MacInnes, 191.

31. Gunn and MacKay, eds., *Sutherland and Reay Country*, 364.

32. Ibid., 366.

Notes to Chapter Two

1. Murray, *The History of the Presbyterian Church in Cape Breton*, 262. Nova Scotia's first Presbyterian open-air communion was held on the west side of Pictou County's Middle River in July 1788. There were no fewer than 130 communicants in attendance; participants

hailed from as far away as Hants County. In later years, Presbyterians from Prince Edward Island numbered among those at MacGregor's communion services. An account of this first service can be found in Patterson, *Memoir of the Rev. James MacGregor,* 158-63, 194-99. *The Pictou Book,* which is composed of a potpourri of excerpts from newspapers and manuscripts, includes a vivid description of a hill-top open-air communion in Pictou in July 1830. The newspaper reporter estimated that the multitude numbered nearly 2,000 participants along with 130 horses. See MacLean, *The Pictou Book,* 221-23.

2. *PW,* 18 August 1855.

3. Ibid., 18 August 1855, 9 August 1856.

4. Ibid., 24 September 1892.

5. Calder, *Communion Memories, The Seven Sayings of the Cross* (see prefactory note).

6. *Sydney Record,* 20 December 1904.

7. In New Annan, Nova Scotia, the Session dictated that those persons in arrears for one year would not be allowed communion privileges until "all arrears are paid up." Maritime Conference Archives, [henceforth MCA], PC-9000/66, Session Register of the New Annan Presbyterian Church and West New Annan United Church 1859-1934, 2 April 1860.

8. MCA, PC-1002#14, Session Minutes, Port Morien, St. John's 1870-1927, 1 October 1887, 49, 17 October 1888, 60.

9. Ibid., 11 March 1903, 21.

10. Schmidt, (2nd edition) 76; Westercamp, *The Triumph of Laity,* 33.

11. *A View of the Whycocomagh Congregation,* 26.

12. "Out door Sacrament" *The Blue Banner,* September 1903, n.p.

13. Watson and Robertson, eds., *Sealladh Gu Taobh,* 14.

14. Interview, Dolly MacKay, Baddeck, 24 May 1995.

15. Cumming et al., *The Story of Framboise,* 113; Interview with Mrs. Kay MacDonald, Blues Mills, 25 September 1995.

16. In Pictou County, Andrew Marshall had little more than porridge to feed the horde of people who stayed at his farm during sacrament week. He saw no need to lavish great expense on his guests, rationalizing his household economies with the quip: "Gin ye are Christians you will be satisfied; and gin ye are no, it's more than you deserve." See Cameron and Macdougall, eds., *One Hundred and Fifty Years in the Life of The First Presbyterian Church (1786-1936),* New Glasgow, Nova Scotia, 161.

17. Nova Scotia Archives and Records Management (henceforth NSARM), Ron Caplan, Recorded interview with Charlie "Holy Malcolm" MacDonald, April 1984.

18. Interview, Mrs. Jessie Morrison, Baddeck, 21 August 1994; Interview, Alexander Smith, Wreck Cove, January 1994.

19. MacPhail, *Loch Bras D'Or*, 44-45; Lavery, *A History of the United Church at Marion Bridge*, Cape Breton, 60.

20. MacPhail, 45.

21. MacLean, *God and the Devil at Seal Cove*, 49-50.

22. Pringle, *Pringle's Mountain*, 58.

23. MacLean, *God and the Devil at Seal Cove*, 50.

24. Phillips, *My Uncle George, The Respectful Recollections of a Backslider in a Highland Manse*, 48.

25. MacPhail, *Loch Bras D'Or*, 44.

26. This information was provided to the author by Mrs. Muriel Kaiser of Baddeck on 15 October 1999. She explained that this sleeping arrangement was commonly used to accommodate guests when they had travelled some distance to attend a public event such as a ship launching and were obliged to stay overnight. She recalled that her own parents first met under such circumstances.

27. Masson,"The Gael in the Far West," *Transactions of the Gaelic Society of Inverness*, 42; Interview, Shamus MacDonald with Dorothy Pottie, Glendale, River Denys Mountain, 24 July 2005. A similar form of ecumenism was manifested in Glengarry County in Eastern Ontario where Roman Catholic neighbours also played host to the Presbyterian pilgrims. According to C. Campbell Fraser,"In the dispensing of this hospitality Roman Catholic neighbours often invited visitors to their homes for Sunday meal. They too felt that this was no ordinary Sunday service which their Protestant friends had to attend." Quoted in MacMillan, *The Kirk in Glengarry*, 412.

28. *PW*, 21 October 1865.

29. Farnham, "Cape Breton Folk," *Harper's New Monthly Magazine*, 624-25.

30. *PW*, 31 July 1897.

31. When Cape-Breton born Angus H. MacLean headed to the Canadian prairies in 1910, he keenly felt the absence of this brand of hospitality. He wrote forlornly, "We walked the town again, and I think we both felt very lonesome for Cape Breton where one could enter a house without knocking, and be sure of a welcome even at

midnight; and where those who did not wish to entertain you would at least make a show of hospitality." MacLean, *The Galloping Gospel*, 13.

32. Morrison, "Religion in old Cape Breton," *Dalhousie Review*, 185.

33. Typescript account of "Sacrament Week" in Baddeck, Provided to the author by Donald Morrison, Baddeck, 21 April 2004.

34. Warner, *Baddeck and that Sort of Thing*, 128.

35. MacDonald, *Group Identity in Social Gatherings: Tradition and Community on the Iona Peninsula*, 186.

36. As early as 1828, Presbyterian clergy in Nova Scotia had their own published primer on communion procedures. *The Directory for the Public Worship of God's Form of Presbyterial Church Government* for 1828 specified that the table should be "decently covered" and "conveniently placed" so that communicants "may orderly sit about it." It was also stipulated that the wine be dispensed "in large cups" and that the bread be contained "in comely and convenient vessels." See p. 23.

37. Interview, Catherine Ross, Blues Mills, 25 September 1995.

38. Interview, Catherine Poole, Whycocomagh, 25 September 1995. Martha Murray of Baddeck also recalled that businesses shut down in the Baddeck area during the communion season. Interview, 24 May 1995.

39. Morrison, "The Early Scotch Settlers of Cape Breton," *The Blue Banner*, June 1904, n.p. There is no evidence that this "fast" was dogmatically observed even in early 19th-century Cape Breton. Furthermore, there is no evidence that the failure to comply ever resulted in the suspension of communion privileges.

40. *PW*, 3 August 1889.

41. Ibid., 24 September 1864.

42. Writing from the vantage point of 1903, the Rev. Alexander Maclean claimed that the Thursday service had once been "held as much more sacred than the Sabbath is now." See *PW*, 21 February 1903.

43. MacMillan, eds., *Reminiscences of the Reverend Alexander Ross*, "Book B," 59; *PW*, 26 December 1874.

44. MacMillan, eds., 59.

45. *PW*, 2 November 1878; "Out door Sacrament," *The Blue Banner*, September 1903, n.p.; *The Blue Banner*, September, 1903, n.p.

46. *PW*, 14 October 1882.

47. Ibid., 24 September 1864.

48. Macmillan, eds., 59.

49. *PW*, 2 August 1889.

50. Morrison, "The Early Scotch Settlers of Cape Breton," *The Blue Banner*, June 1904, n.p. See also "La na Ceist air an Eilean Mhor," *The Blue Banner*, September 1905, n.p.

51. *Ecclesiastical and Missionary Record of Free Church of Nova-Scotia*, December 1855, 187.

52. PW, 23 August 1890.

53. Ibid., 27 September 1890.

54. MacInnes, "The Origin and Early Development of the 'Men,'" *Records of the Scottish Church History Society*, 16-41; Innes, "The Religion of the Highlands," *The British and Foreign Evangelical Review*, vol XXI, (July, 1872) 413-46; Kennedy, *The Days of the Fathers in Ross-shire*, 73-105; Beaton, *Some Noted Ministers of the Northern Highlands*, 1929; Bruce, "Social Change and Collective Behaviour: the Revival in Eighteenth Century Ross-shire," *The British Journal of Sociology*, 567-68.

55. MacInnes, 97-220. See also Hunter, *The Making of the Crofting Community*, 96, 105; and MacRae, *Revivals in the Highlands and Islands in the 19th Century*.

56. MacInnes, 215.

57. *PW*, 6 December 1851.

58. Beaton, "Fast Day and Friday Fellowship Meeting Controversy in the Synod of Sutherland and Caithness (1737-1758)," *Transactions of the Gaelic Society of Inverness*, 159-82. The Rev. J. S. Mackay of Fort Augustus, Scotland, wrote disparagingly of "the Men" in the 1890s. He decried their lack of education, noting with ill-concealed contempt that their "zeal outran their knowledge, and they became filled too high with their own importance." The Ceist, he claimed, had degenerated into an outlet for "all manner of rivalries and jealousies" and permitted unseemly displays of ignorance on "frivolous or ill-stated" questions. The Men, he alleged, were given license to "harangue" and "ramble" on with "their undigested stuff" without the "control, correction or direction" of the clergy. See Gunn and Mackay, 355.

59. MacInnes, 214.

60. The Presbyterian Church in Scotland has a long history of factionalism centring most notably on the issue of the Church's independence vis-à-vis the state. One of the most celebrated splinter groups was the Free Church of Scotland which was spawned by the defection of over 450 clerics who broke away from their parent church during the Disruption of 1843.

61. *The Home and Foreign Missionary Record for the Church of Scotland,* (January, 1857) 12. The members of the Deputation responded initially with revulsion to the Ceist: "Previous to our witnessing this interesting spectacle, we confess we cherished rooted prejudice against such systematised lay instruction, as being fraught with danger to the peace of congregations and being a great provocation to spiritual pride." Pictou County clergyman, Rev. A. Maclean admitted that the doctrinal knowledge of these "sainted Patriarchs" was often intimidating to the neophyte clergyman. Alexander Urquhart, a well-known catechist in Pictou County, was such a gifted speaker that his Ceist-day orations

> made the young minister, new to these Friday meetings, not a little nervous. He, the presiding minister, had no time to study the passage, no help from commentary, no notes available. It was a trying experience for a young man. The passage was given then and there, and perhaps not one he had ever carefully examined, but there was no escape. He must stand up in the crowded church—crowded as it always was on that Friday—and do the best he could, with the result not seldom that Urquhart and others have left him some distance behind.

See Maclean, *The Story of the Kirk in Nova Scotia,* 48-9.

62. *PW,* 16 August 1913.

63. Ibid., 8 September 1900 and 18 May 1901. M. D. Morrison also testified to their profound impact on young impressionable minds, summoning from his boyhood memories, "vivid recollections of one or two of these men … and of the sense of adoration that overwhelmed me as one succeeded the other in throwing the multitude into ecstatic raptures." Another extraordinary feature was the "affection" that they commanded from young people during much of the 19th century: "Some how they mastered the secret of influencing the young." See Morrison, "Religion in old Cape Breton," *Dalhousie Review,* 189

64. *PW,* 8 September 1900.

65. Ibid., 14 September 1889.

66. MacPhail, *Cape Breton,* n.p., c.1932, 17.

67. Morrison "The Early Scotch Settlers," n.p.

68. MacPhail, *Loch Bras D'Or,* 45.

69. Ibid.

70. Ibid.

71. Interview, Sadie MacInnis (interviewed by Shamus MacDonald) North Shore, 4 August 2005.

72. *PW*, 27 September 1890.

73. In October 1894, the Rev. M. A. McKenzie, who travelled to Cape North to attend the induction of the Rev. Malcolm McLeod, applauded the demure mien of the local women at the Ceist. He wrote approvingly, "The women seemed to cultivate that modesty and decorum which the Apostle characterizes as the only real beauty." See *PW*, 6 October 1894.

74. It is interesting to note that within their own religious organizations, Cape Breton Presbyterian women demonstrated force and spirit. The notations of the Malagawatch branch of the Women's Missionary Society, established on 8 July 1897, have a somewhat belligerent tone.

> At one of the meetings Mrs. Rose expressed a desire to have more of the members present at the meetings. Someone explained that the reason was that there was a certain amount of prejudice against our meetings. Not so much among the women as among the men—one man having asked, "Do the women really pray at your meetings?" Our advice to such minded men is to come to our meetings and see for themselves that we do nothing, to cause us to be ashamed.

See MCA, PC-302 #1, River and Lakeside Presbyterian Church, Historical Sketch of Malagawatch WMS 1897-1947, 5.

75. Interview, Catherine Ross, Blues Mills, 25 September 1995.

76. Murray, 268.

77. *The Ecclesiastical and Missionary Record of the Free Church of Nova-Scotia*, December 1855, 187.

78. *PW*, 18 December 1858.

79. Ibid., 6 October 1894.

80. NSARM, MGI 1471 A, Diary of the Rev. Murdoch Stewart. The Rev. John Murray confessed that his first meeting with Angus McLean of Cape North was somewhat disconcerting and challenging. Murray recalled:

> all at once he broke in with: "Have you been sowing seed yourself since you came to the place?" in Gaelic. I was surprised at the question and did not know how to take it at first, but he soon made it clear that the question was intended in the spiritual sense. Gradually it dawned on

me that my interlocutor could be no other than the Angus McLean of whom I had heard so much from my predecessors in Cape North—William Grant and Samuel Gunn. So I brushed up my mystical theology and talked to him as best I could....

Quoted in Malcolm Campbell, *Cape Breton Worthies*, 32.

81. *MacTalla*, 24 June 1904.

82. *PW*, 8 September 1900.

83. Where relevant, it was customary for obituaries in the *Presbyterian Witness* to record some mention of the contributions that the deceased made as a Ceist-day participant.

84. A. Bain to M. Campbell, 23 March 1911, quoted in Campbell, 29; *The Ecclesiastical and Missionary Record of the Free Church of Nova-Scotia*, April 1854, 27.

85. Charles Dunn, *Highland Settler*, 98.

86. *MacTalla*, vol 12, no 24, 1904. I am grateful to Effie Rankin who brought this reference to my attention and to Michael Linkletter who translated the lengthy elegy for me. The following is a brief excerpt from the effusive tribute.

> A messenger came to get you
> Who didn't take pity on your young children,
> Who left them like sheep on a mountain,
> Raised on the words of your mouth;
> It left them without a leader or a guide
> To draw them to the store
> In which there was plenitude without decrease,
> And from which you were wont to pour into their mouths.

87. *PW*, 2 November 1878, 8 September 1900.

88. Campbell, 21; Murray, 261.

89. *PW*, 31 August 1878.

90. *PW*, 8 September 1900.

91. Ibid., 3 March 1894.

92. Ibid., 1 August 1903.

93. Ibid., 19 April 1879, 8 September 1900.

94. Ibid.

95. Campbell, 23.

96. Beaton Institute archives (henceforth BIA), MG 12, 219.A "Donald Macdonald" (typescript by Estelle Jean Worfolk) 1940.

97. *PW*, 16 April 1904.

98. *A View of the Congregation of Whycocomagh*, 37.

99. Campbell, 27-8.

100. *PW*, 14 October 1882.

101. Campbell, 28.

102. MacKenzie, "Cape Breton Worthies" *The Canadian-American Gael*, vol 1, 1944, 88.

103. Ibid.

104. Ibid., vol 2, c.1948, p. 15.

105. Ibid.

106. Ibid., vol 1, 88.

107. Thornhill and MacDonald, eds., *The Road to Tarbot*, 79.

108. Ibid., 83.

109. John Murray to Malcolm Campbell, 22 October 1910, quoted in Campbell, 29, 31.

110. *PW*, 8 September 1900.

111. *The Edinburgh Christian Instructor and Colonial Religious Register*, vol 3 (March 1840) New Series, 116.

112. Under exceptional circumstances, new members could be admitted to "full communion" as late as Sunday morning. The examination process of regular communicants was not restricted to Saturday. In fact, it continued throughout the five-day period.

113. MCA, PC-1002#14, Port Morien, St. John's Session Minutes 1870-1927, 13 June 1891, 74.

114. Easthouse, *Settlers of Southside: St. George's Channel*, Nova Scotia. n.p., 1975, 104.

115. Ibid.

116. Ibid.

117. MCA, PC-305#3, Session Minutes, West Bay 1898-1959, 9 July 1898, 6.

118. Ibid., PC-305#1, Register of Communicants, West Bay, Cape Breton 1871-1925.

119. It is widely believed that communion tokens in the form of stamped cards were introduced in Scotland shortly after the Reformation. Although the conventional metal token, fashioned from lead (or less commonly from tin, brass or pewter) soon gained popularity, the use of the terminology "tickets" persisted. See Wright, Lachman, and Meek, *Dictionary of Scottish Church History & Theology* 200.

120. Vickery, "Communion tokens" *Collections of the Royal Nova Scotia Historical Society*, 155-73. According to Vickery, by 1938 experts had located at least 241 varieties of communion tokens which had been used in Canada; 69 of these were identified with Nova Scotia.

121. BIA, MG13 135(A), Meetings of the Session, Deaths, Records of Baptism, Marriages … 1899-1936, East Lake Ainslie Presbyterian Church

122. MacLean, *God and the Devil at Seal Cove*, 52.

123. Even one's demeanour and style of speech were transformed to reflect sober preparation for the Sabbath. It is said that in Gairloch, Nova Scotia, "all frivolous talk" was to cease by five o'clock on Saturday. One anecdote illustrates the scrupulosity with which the Sabbath rule was observed:

> The writer can remember one Sun. after church services John McPherson, an aged man, who lived a strict Christian life, called in for a few minutes, and my father asked why his son Donald was absent from the service, and the old patriarch replied that "Donald had gone to Truro on business, whereof it is not lawful to speak on the Sabbath day." On Monday we found that he was away getting a machine to pull stumps out of the ground.

See *The Eastern Chronicle* (New Glasgow), 28 May 1935.

Jane MacKay Rutherford's reminiscences confirm the unwillingness of older Pictou County Presbyterians to discuss their Monday plans on a Sunday. See Rutherford, *I came from Pictou County, The Recollections of Jane MacKay Rutherford*, 8.

124. The attitude that Sunday should be inviolable could go to moralistic extremes. Jane MacKay Rutherford's reminiscences recount the tragic story of a young Campbell woman from Pictou County who was drowned on a Sunday when she went to collect leeches to help treat her sister's medical condition. She was later buried in the dress she had woven for her hope chest. Local residents grimly rationalized that she had been the witting author of her own fate. Rutherford writes, "Later the whispers went round—the girl was drowned, but after all, she had gone out for leeches on a Sunday, the Lord's Day." Rutherford, 9.

125. Easthouse, 103-104.

126. Caplan, "Hattie Carmichael of the Meadow Road," *Cape Breton's Magazine*, 8.

127. Pringle, 121.

128. Sabbatarianism was enforced with similar vigor among Pictou County Presbyterians. Jane MacKay Rutherford recalled that "It was a shocking thing, too, to see anyone clean his nails on the Sabbath." Rutherford, 8. The Sabbath ban against cutting one's hair or nails was widely practised in Scotland. See Elizabeth Fay Shaw's *Folksongs and Folklore of South Uist*. Aberdeen: Aberdeen University Press, 1955 cited in MacDonald, *Cultural Retention and Adaptation among the Highland Scots of Carolina*, 86, 94ff. The staid tone of the Sabbath notwithstanding, children in Lewis must have relished the fact that parents did not mete out punishment on Sunday. The day of reckoning for misbehaviour was postponed until Monday, the so-called "*Di-luain à bhreabain*"—"the Monday of the kicking." This day was aptly named for the children usually kicked their feet as they protested against the enforcement of physical discipline. See MacDonald, 86.

129. NSARM, MG 1, vol 745, no. 43, M. McDonald to "dear William," 3 June 1885.

130. Ibid.

131. Ibid.

132. MacLean, *God and the Devil at Seal Cove*, 52.

133. MacDonald, *Echoes of the Past*, 87.

134. *The Ecclesiastical and Missionary Record of the Free Church of Nova Scotia*, September 1855, 165; *PW*, 21 October 1865; *The Cape-Breton News*, 8 September 1852. Similar feats of dogged devotion and physical stamina were recorded in Pictou County where visitors to the Gairloch communion came from as far afield as Cape Breton. It is recorded that Angus Sutherland, even at the advanced years of 102, travelled on foot from his home to the sacrament in Pictou, a distance of twenty miles each way. See The Eastern Chronicle, 28 May 1935.

135. *PW*, 5 April 1902.

136. Ibid., 23 November 1901.

137. BIA, MG14, 158 F, "Progress of Cape Breton in 100 years" 13 September 1904.

138. BIA, MG 13, 85 (microfilm), Knox Presbyterian Church, Boularderie 1875-1904, 131-32.

139. MacMillan, "Book B," 59.

140. "Out door sacrament," n.p.

141. Typescript account of "Sacrament Week" in Baddeck; PW, 28 September 1918.

142. *PW*, 13 September 1884.

143. Interview, Mrs. Jessie Morrison, Baddeck, 21 August 1994; Interview, Miss Marion MacNeil, Ainslie Glen, 5 September 1994.

144. It is interesting to note that school registers often attributed class absenteeism to the lack of adequate footwear among students.

145. Schmidt, "'A Church-going People are a Dress-loving People': Clothes, Communication, and Religious Culture in Early America," 45.

146. Schmidt, (1st edition) 95.

147. *PW*, 24 November 1883.

148. *The Ecclesiastical and Missionary Record*, August 1856, 63.

149. *PW*, 17 August 1889.

150. Ibid., 9 October 1852.

151. Ibid., 17 August 1889.

152. *The Cape-Breton News*, 8 September 1852; Jack, "Pioneer Days of the Church of the Elders in Cape Breton," *The Blue Banner*, October 1905, n.p.

153. *MacTalla*, 1 September 1894.

154. Interview, Mrs. Catherine Ross, Blues Mills, 25 September 1995.

155. *Home and Foreign Missionary Record for the Church of Scotland*, January 1842-December 1844, 204.

156. *PW*, 9 October 1852. It is interesting to note that *The Cape-Breton News* for 8 September 1852 published conflicting estimates, reckoning a crowd of no larger than 2,500 to 3,000.

157. Ibid., 9 October 1852.

158. Ibid., 29 October 1853. Some estimates are even more generous. At least two *Presbyterian Witness* articles, published more than forty years after the event, cite the figure of 10,000. See *Presbyterian Witness*, 30 April 1898 and 14 October 1899.

159. Ibid., 14 October 1899.

160. Ibid.

161. MacMillan, *The Kirk in Glengarry*, 10.

162. *PW*, 18 August 1855, 9 August 1856.

163. Ibid., 21 October 1865.

164. Ibid., 27 September 1890, 24 September 1892.

165. Farnham, 620.

166. MacMillan, "Book B," 55.

167. *PW*, 21 October 1865.

168. Farnham, 625.

169. Masson, 42.

170. MacPhail, *Loch Bras d'Or*, 44.

171. This is in marked contrast with the attire of African-Nova Scotian women at mid-19th-century summer baptisms in Dartmouth, Preston and Lawrencetown. There the dress code sanctioned "parasols, hoopskirts, sash-ribbons, veils & fans." See Janet Guildford's "The Role of Women in the Urban Middle Class Household Economy, Halifax, Nova Scotia, 1840-1880," 14. Schmidt argues that communion season attire was customarily new, even made specifically for the event. However, I can find no parallel in Cape Breton until the late 19th century. See Schmidt (1st edition), 81. Anglican church-going attire was dramatically different judging from Burrows W. Sleigh's description of the gaily-dressed parishioners at a mid-19th-century Sunday service in Sydney, Cape Breton. The congregation, he observed, "presented a vista of young and elderly ladies, very flashily dressed, with airs of considerable pride and conceit." See Tennyson, ed., *Impressions of Cape Breton*, 129.

172. *Home and Foreign Missionary Record*, vol 1, July 1835-December 1841, 405.

173. Letter from A. Munro to Rev. Alexander Farquharson, 1 January 1883 quoted in Archibald, "Early Scottish Settlers in Cape Breton," *Collections of the Nova Scotia Historical Society*, 96.

174. Archibald, 91.

175. *PW*, 20 August 1910.

176. Ibid., 1 October 1864.

177. Ibid.

178. Ibid.

179. Latimer, *Local History of Orangedale and Surrounding Area*, n.p.

180. Warner, 123.

181. Perrot, *Fashioning the Bourgeoisie*, 30, 32. Leigh Schmidt states that clothing, invested with manifold meanings relating to age, social status, political authority and gender, also served as an important medium of visual communication in the religious culture of early America. In short, rules about dress contain doctrinal and spiritual significance. Schmidt notes that among the Quakers, pietists and evangelicals "plain dress became a central expression of social and religious protest" and projected a potentially "subversive message" by linking "simplicity with virtue" and "plainness with godliness," promoting a more egalitarian religious culture and challenging the elite's "pageantry of hierarchy." Plainness in dress also became a device for distinguishing the boundaries between saved and un-

saved as well as inclusion and exclusion. In short, it helped define membership and reinforce a sense of distinct community. Schmidt, "'A Church-going People'," 36, 38, 40-41

182. Perrot, 30, 32.

183. Neville and Westerhoff, *Learning through Liturgy*, 3-4. According to Neville, the use of a natural setting and the emphasis on nature as an aspect of religious experience were deeply rooted in the Celtic tradition of the sacred grove.

184. *Guardian* (Halifax), 13 January 1841.

185. *PW*, 11 March 1865.

186. Ibid.

187. Ibid., 27 August 1853.

188. Ibid., 27 September 1890; *The Ecclesiastical and Missionary Record of the Free Church of Nova-Scotia*, September 1855, 165. The meeting sites for Methodist camp meetings were also imbued with sacred meaning. They became the keystone of Methodist spirituality and were held out-of-doors, invariably in some "picturesque setting," which was sanctified by God's presence. They too served as vehicles for religious conversion and renewal and were enjoyed as a type of "spiritual vacation." See Cooley, "Manna and the Manual: Sacramental and Instructive Constructions of the Victorian Methodist Camp Meeting during the mid-Nineteenth Century," *Religion and American Culture*, 131-59 and Clements, "The Physical Layout of the Methodist Camp Meeting," *Pioneer America*, 9-15.

189. *Ecclesiastical and Missionary Record of the Free Church of Nova-Scotia*, (October 1855) 170.

190. *PW*, 21 October 1865.

191. Ibid.

192. D. McMillan, *The History of Presbyterianism in Cape Breton*. Sydney: Sydney Printing Co., Ltd., 1904, 46.

193. *PW*, 17 August 1889.

194. Masson, 42.

195. *PW*, 28 August 1897.

196. Ibid., 18 December 1858, 28 July 1894; Robert F. Burns, *The Life and Times of the Rev. Robert Burns*, DD, Toronto: James Campbell & Son, 1873, 323.

197. Ibid., 22 September 1860, 1 October 1864, 27 August 1853.

198. The same phenomenon operated in Pictou County. For example, the site of the summer communions for the members of St. Columba church was regarded with "peculiar awe." According to the Rev. A. M.

MacLeod, "It is a sacred spot to many, not only to those who live in the community, but also to a great host of others who live in almost every part of this continent." See MacLeod, *History of St. Columba Church*, 9.

199. "The Late Rev. Murdoch Buchanan," *The Blue Banner*, May 1905, n.p.

200. *PW*, 24 September 1864.

201. MacMillan, "Book B," 59.

202. Ibid.

203. Hyde and Bird, *Hallowed Timbers: The Wooden Churches of Cape Breton*, 25.

204. BIA, Session book of Boularderie Kirk Session 1875-1904, 3 July 1882, 35.

205. There were apparently slight architectural variations in these structures. According to Mrs. Catherine MacAskill of Boularderie, "St. James' tent was a little more detailed in design than that of Knox." Rev. Ritchie Robinson to author, 18 October 1994.

206. MacPhail, 46; *A View of the Whycocomagh Congregation*, 26; Pringle, 57.

207. *The Ecclesiastical and Missionary Record of the Free Church of Nova-Scotia*, (September 1855), 165.

208. Johnston, "'Ticket to Heaven': the Rise and Fall of the Communion Token," *The Canadian Society of Presbyterian Historical Society Papers*, 18.

209. Typescript account of "Sacrament Week" in Baddeck.

210. Nicholson et al., *Middle River*, 67.

211. *PW*, 1 October 1864.

212. BIA, Vertical File, "Presbyterian Church and Clergy," Cape Bretoner, 5 April 1958.

213. Mrs. Catherine MacAskill of Boularderie recalls that there was a tin offering plate nailed on a stump outside St. James "for some years." Rev. Ritchie Robinson to author, 18 October 1994.

214. Morrison, "Religion in Old Cape Breton," 189.

215. *PW*, 1 October 1864.

216. Ibid.

217. Farnham, 625.

218. Ibid.

219. *PW*, 18 May 1901.

220. MCA, PC-305#3, Session Minutes, West Bay 1898-1959, 26 June 1914, 48.

221. Farnham, 623.

222. Schmidt, (1st edition) 89.

223. Grant, "Brands from Blazing Heather: Canadian Religious Revival in the Highland Tradition,"*The Canadian Society of Presbyterian History Papers*, 61.

224. Ibid.

225. Quoted in Grant, 62.

226. The Rev. James MacGregor of Pictou County enjoyed comparable celebrity as an extraordinary preacher. His powerful voice was described variously as "rather plaintive and tender" and "beautifully clear and melodious as a woman's." Some contemporaries alleged that his voice could project half a mile, "where not only was his voice heard, but the words were distinguished." Patterson, 198

227. *PW*, 29 October 1853, 16 May 1868.

228. McMillan, 14.

229. See, for example, *PW*, 16 February 1901 and 17 December 1904.

230. MCA, PC-1006#15, Mira-Union Presbyterian Church Session Minutes 1874-1884, 5 October 1882, 28-29.

231. *PW*, 7 October 1849, 6 February 1886.

232. Ibid., 28 August 1897.

233. Ibid., 10 November 1883; Photocopied samples of several of McLeod's sermons (at least one is a communion sermon) can be seen at BIA, MG 13, 100, Rev. Hugh McLeod's Sermons 1797-1877. The Rev. D. McMillan waxed enthusiastically about McLeod's charismatic style of preaching, writing "I still hear those ringing notes, those piercing sentences, that voice which could be heard to the fullest limit of the congregation." See McMillan, 46.

234. *PW*, 10 November 1883.

235. Ibid., 21 August 1858, 27 January 1894

236. MacMillan, "Book B," 10-11.

237. Murray, 119.

238. McMillan, 23.

239. MCA, Box PP 301, Minutes of the Presbytery of Inverness, 11 May 1909, 220.

240. Wright, Lachman & Meek, 671

241. Ibid.

242. Ibid.

243. Dunn, 94. According to Dunn, the Presbyterian settlers referred to these memorable words of spiritual wisdom as "notes."

244. *PW*, 18 August 1855.

245. Ibid.

246. Ibid., 27 September 1890.

247. Ibid., 22 September 1860.

248. Morrison, "Religion in Old Cape Breton," 188.

249. Farnham, 625.

250. *The Ecclesiastical and Missionary Record of the Free Church of Nova-Scotia*, July 1856, 56; *The Monthly Record of the Church of Scotland*, November 1872, 263.

251. Westerkamp, 162. One anecdote from Pictou County illustrates how opinionated Scottish Presbyterians were about the preaching talents of their clergy. Certainly, they had no compunctions about verbalizing their opinions. One Pictou County resident, after weighing the merits of two respected ministers, stated: "Ah! I would rather listen to Dr. MacGregor's voice without words than Mr. A's preaching." See Cameron and Macdougall, 63. One visitor to Cape Breton in 1889 was struck by the "critical spirit," partisanship and judgmental nature of its Presbyterian residents. As one example, he described an exchange with a church-goer who was particularly parsimonious with his praise: "I ventured to say to a stalwart Highlander that the sermon was excellent. He stroked his beard, shrugged his shoulders and replied indifferently, "'Aye, no 'sae bud, for him.'" See Elliott, "A Nineteenth Century Tourist in Cape Breton," *Journal of Education*, 25.

252. Cairns et al., 73; Henderson, *Scotland: Kirk and People*, 27-31.

253. *PW*, 16 September 1865, 9 July 1870. The Presbyterian Witness also held the opinion that Cape Breton Presbyterians set high standards for their preachers, writing "they want ministers who can preach well in English and Gaelic; that ministers who would please them are hard to find." See PW, 14 October 1882. George Patterson contended that linguistic loyalties to Gaelic ran so deep that some early Nova Scotia Presbyterians deliberately relocated to Pictou so that "they might be under the ministry of Doctor MacGregor and enjoy the gospel in their native tongue." Patterson, 201.

254. *The Presbytyerian Record*, January 1896, 7-8; See also Elliott, 25. Dr. MacGregor identified another interesting distinction in the tastes and preferences of his Gaelic-speaking and English-speaking audiences. He observed, "But the Highlanders wanted the action-sermon, and the Lowlanders the evening sermon." Patterson, 160.

126

255. MacLeod, *History of St. Columba Church*, 13. For further details about the tokens, see McLachlan, *Canadian Communion Tokens*; Bowman, *Communion Tokens of the Presbyterian Church in Canada*; MacLennan, *The Story of the Old Time Communion Service and Worship*; and Shiells, *The Story of the Token*.

256. BIA, MG13, 100, Rev. H. McLeod's Sermons, 1797-1877.

257. MCA, F & I, Box 63, #149, Rev. Matthew Wilson's Communion Sermons 1869-1880.

258. MacMillan, "Book B," 13; It is not clear how and when Cape Breton Presbyterian congregations managed to obtain the vessels required for the communion service especially in view of their early financial straits. It is possible that some congregations borrowed what they needed from more established churches. Certainly that was the case at the first sacrament in Gairloch, Pictou County, where West Branch, now St. Columba, came "to their aid and loaned them theirs for the occasion." See Hawkins et al., *Gairloch, Pictou County, Nova Scotia*, 89.

259. Schmidt, (1st edition) 100.

260. MacLean, *God and the Devil at Seal Cove*, 46.

261. *PW*, 1 October 1864.

262. MacMillan, "Book B," 59.

263. MacLean, *God and the Devil at Seal Cove*, 46.

264. Schmidt, (2nd edition) 197.

265. MCA, PC-9000/66, Session Register of New Annan Presbyterian Church and West New Annan United Church, 1859-1934, 28 July 1860. At one Session, the elders stipulated that residual wine after the communion could not be sold. However, a "sick person" could be given "a little gratuitously." Unfortunately, there is also little information about the number of bushels of wheat required to prepare the bread for the communion. It is, however, recorded that during the lean years in Cape Breton, the farmers saved their small surplus of wheat to produce the communion bread.

266. MCA, F & I, Box 63 #149. Rev. Matthew Wilson's Communion Sermons 1869-1880.

267. BIA, MG13, 100, Rev. H. McLeod's Sermons, 1797-1877.

268. *PW*, 29 October 1853.

269. *MacTalla*, 1 September 1894.

270. Dunn, 96.

271. It is unclear whether Cape Breton Presbyterian congregations were strife-ridden by the often divisive conflict over the use of the

tuning fork or pitch pipe. The use of these instruments ignited debate in some Pictou County congregations. In 1836, for example, the Pictou Presbytery resolved that "Having heard commissioners for and against the pitch pipe, [they] were unanimously of opinion that the use of the pitch pipe ought in the meantime to be discontinued. Both parties expressed themselves as perfectly satisfied." Thirteen years later, "singers were granted the use of the Pitch Pipe." See Cameron and Macdougall, 72. The Rev. A. M. MacLeod suggests that the failure to use a tuning fork sometimes had discordant consequences. The music, he notes, "was often spoiled by the high pitch on which it was sung." See MacLeod, *History of St. Columba Church*, 12.

272. EdinburghGuide.com—Celtic Connections News, 21 January 2005.

273. Caplan, "Gaelic Precenting on the North Shore," *Cape Breton's Magazine*, 45-49. See also Patterson, 199-200. The Rev. George Patterson, grandson of the Rev. James MacGregor, recalled Nova Scotia's precenting tradition with dewy-eyed nostalgia, writing: "But we must especially notice the singing. Who that has heard the service of praise at a Highland sacrament at the present day can have forgotten it? The old tunes, all in the minor key, with their peculiar mournful expression.

> 'Perhaps Dundee's wild warbling measures rise,
> Or plaintive Martyrs, worthy of the name,
> Or noble Elgin beets the heavenward flame,
> The sweetest far of Scotia's holy lays,
> Compared with these, Italian trills are tame,
> Nae unison ha'e they with our Creator's praise.'

274. Fergusson, *Beyond the Hebrides: Including the Cape Breton Collection*, 271.

275. MacKenzie, "The Precentor as an Institution, Next to the Home, in Making a Major Contribution to the Promotion and Preservation of the Gaelic Language" *The Canadian-American Gael*, vol 1, 1944, 89. The interplay between the Presbyterian order of service, music and communion sacrament is examined in Bynum, "'The Genuine Presbyterian Whine': Presbyterian Worship in the Eighteenth Century," *American Presbyterians*, 157-70.

276. Wood, *The Tourist's Maritime Provinces*, 224.

277. Ibid.

278. Campbell, ed., *The Little Church by the Lake: A History of the Alexander Grant Memorial United Church*, 86.

279. Lavery, 17, 21.

280. *PW*, 31 December 1910.

281. MCA, PP 1001, Records of the Presbytery of Sydney 1896-1908, 13 March 1900, 75-76.

282. *PW*, 27 August 1853.

283. Ibid., 10 September 1853.

284. *Cape Breton News*, 27 October 1852.

285. T*he Home and Foreign Record*, (July 1838 – December 1841), vol 1, 406.

286. *Monthly Record of Church of Scotland*, November 1872, 261-62.

287. *PW*, 4 March 1871.

288. Ibid.

289. Ibid.

290. Ibid., 4 March 1871.

291. Ibid.

292. MCA, PC-1002#14, Session Minutes, St. John's Presbyterian Church, Port Morien, 1870-1927, 1 January 1871, 10.

293. *The Edinburgh Christian Instructor and Colonial Religious Register*, March 1840, vol 3, n.s., 116; *Home and Foreign Missionary Record*, July 1839-December 1841, 167; *PW*, September 1855.

294. *Ecclesiastical and Missionary Record of the Free Church of Nova-Scotia*, (July 1857), 54.

295. Ibid., (September 1858) 70.

296. BIA, MG13, 100, Rev. McLeod's Sermons 1797-1877.

297. *PW*, 21 January 1871.

298. Ibid.

299. Ibid., 4 March 1871.

300. "Statistics," *The Blue Banner*, June 1904, n.p.

301. MacPhail, *Loch Bras D'Or*, 46.

302. *PW*, 21 October 1865.

303. *The Monthly Record of the Church of Scotland*, November 1872, 261

304. *PW*, 14 September 1889.

305. Rev. R. A. Arnold to the Lord Bishop of Nova Scotia, 29 March 1853. Quoted in Stanley, *The Well-Watered Garden: The Presbyterian Church in Cape Breton*, 1798-1860, 145.

306. McInnes, 220. The Rev. Alexander McLeod of Lewis, Scotland, also applied stringent rules of admission to his communions. Admittance to communion was so restricted that a communion roll

that boasted 800 to 900 communicants before 1824 was reduced to nine. McLeod's debarring or "table fencing" practices reached such extremes that his co-Presbyterian from the parish of Knock, the Rev. Duncan Matheson, remarked: "he debarred everyone in the Congregation....He debarred me, and my opinion is that he debarred himself at last."The Rev. Roderick McLeod of Skye was cut from the same cloth. Like many Free Church evangelicals he believed that the "Moderates" had administered both communion and baptism indiscriminately so that the parishioners were "for a long course of years accustomed to receive sealing ordinances, without the least regard to knowledge, or to moral character."The communion roll in Bracadale was dramatically curtailed under McLeod's pastorate, reduced from 150 communicants to ten. In short, communion was placed above general attainment and narrowly restricted to the virtuous, those of "rare Christian attainment." See *The First Annual Report of the Society for the Support of Gaelic Schools with an appendix respecting the present state of the Highlands and Islands of Scotland & etc.* citing letter from the Rev. Thomas Ross, 7 Jan. 1811, 15; Henderson, *The Scottish Ruling Elder*, 66; MacRae, 18; MacDermid, 268-69; and MacDonald, *Social and Religious Life in the Highlands*, 98.

307. *The Presbyterian Witness* elaborated on this point, writing "It is sad to think that there are individuals who are disposed to take credit to themselves because they have never joined in the solemn service of communion—individuals who, while chargeable with the guilt of neglecting the Saviour's dying command, are yet cherishing in their own hearts a certain feeling of complacence, because they are free, as they think, from the obligations which are laying on the professing disciples of Christ." See *PW*, 5 May 1883.

308. Ross, *An Address to The Members of The Presbyterian Church of Nova Scotia*, 4, 6-7.

309. *PW*, 10 March 1888.

310. Ibid., 9 May 1863. This situation diverges dramatically from Leigh Schmidt's findings that the average age of first-time communicants in late 18th-century Scotland and America was generally fifteen or sixteen years. But there was considerable flexibility on this point, for it was not uncommon for children as young as twelve to seek admission to the Lord's table. See Schmidt, (1st edition) 84.

311. *PW*, 18 May 1901.

312. Ibid., 30 September 1899.

313. MacPhail, *Loch Bras D'Or*, 46.

314. This singular attitude towards the sacrament of the Lord's Supper continued to distress church leaders in the Highlands well into the 1960s. See *The Lord's Supper: An Appeal to the People of the Church of Scotland in the Highlands and Islands*.

315. MacLean, *God and the Devil at Seal Cove*, 46.

316. Ibid.

317. MacMillan, "Book A," 31.

318. Ibid.

319. *PW*, 20 September 1890. See also 27 August 1853.

320. *The Monthly Record of the Church of Scotland*, November 1872, 260.

321. Maclean, *The Story of the Kirk in Nova Scotia*, 77. The Rev. Maclean recalled that at his first communion he was "much pleased at my success in getting through the whole work at 3 o'clock. I suspect it was the first time the Gaelic service was closed at so early an hour." Ross learned quickly, however, that this accomplishment was no cause for boast. In fact, it soon became clear that, owing to youthful inexperience, he had unwittingly committed an error in judgment and shortchanged the congregation with his hurried dispensation of communion.

322. *PW*, 14 October 1882.

323. Schmidt, (1st edition) 86.

324. Cumming et al., 114.

325. Ferguson et al., *Pride in the Past: Faith in the Future: A History of the Stewart United Church, 1893-1993*, 43.

326. Cumming et al., 113.

327. *Victoria-Inverness Bulletin*, 23 November 1929

328. *The Daily Telegraph* (Saint John), 19 September 1874.

329. *PW*, 8 August 1891.

330. Ibid., 5 December 1857.

331. MacMillan, "Book B," 60.

332. *PW*, 30 April 1898; 14 October 1899.

333. Ibid., 6 October 1866.

Notes on Chapter Three

1. "Pre-Communion Service" *The Blue Banner*, December 1905, n.p.

2. *The Home and Foreign Record of the Presbyterian Church of the Lower Provinces of British North America*, December 1862, 329.

3. Ibid., June 1875, 175.

4. MCA, PC-1002#14, Session Minutes, Port Morien, St. John's Presbyterian Church, 1870-1927, 19 March 1904, 109, 124. By 1908, Port Morien celebrated quarterly communions. See entry for 19 August 1908.

5. According to James M. Cameron, the last outdoor communion services in Pictou County were held at Hopewell and Gairloch in the 1880s. See Cameron, *Enduring Trust: First Presbyterian Church, New Glasgow, Nova Scotia, 1786-1986*, 18. In his book, *Holy Fairs*, Schmidt documents the decline of open-air sacramental gatherings in the Scottish Lowlands and the United States, and concludes that by the 1850s this tradition had been pushed to the periphery. It should be noted that Schmidt neglects to discuss the vibrant persistence of this institution in the Scottish Highlands. See Schmidt, 206.

6. Ibid., 24 July 1897.

7. *PW*, 3 August 1889.

8. Ibid., 3 October 1896.

9. Lavery, 60.

10. *The Blue Banner*, October 1903, n.p.

11. *MacTalla*, 1 September 1894.

12. *The Blue Banner*, October 1903, n.p. According to "Cape North," *The Blue Banner* (September 1903), this same pattern emerged in Cape North.

13. Mervyn MacAulay to author, 11 September 1994; Rev. Ritchie Robinson to author, 6 October 1994. These details were extracted from *Minutes of Meetings of Session of Boularderie Congregation from July 21st*, 1905 to April 6th, 1969.

14. *PW*, 4 August 1888.

15. "The Pre-Communion Service," *The Blue Banner,* December 1905, n.p.

16. *PW*, 14 September 1895, 20 July 1895. As late as 1903, Cape North and Grand River continued to practice the classic five-day Sàcramaid. The Rev. Donald MacDonald, minister at Strathlorne, defended this more prolonged version of the communion season in a *Blue Banner* article entitled "Comanachadh Gaidhealach." He challenged those critics who regarded even the three-day format as "excessive" with the refutation that that these additional days were required in order that the communicants consider in full measure their own worth and

the magnitude of Christ's sacrifice. T*he Blue Banner* (August 1903) n.p.

17. MacMillan,"Book B,"59.

18. MCA, PC-300#2, Session Minutes, Margaree, 24 August 1907, 39.

19. Sack, *Whitebread Protestants: Food and Religion in American Culture*, 49.

20. *PW*, 20 December 1906. New Glasgow was one of the first places in Canada to adopt individual cups. See McNeil, *The Presbyterian Church in Canada, 1875-1925*, 215.

21. MCA, PC-1002#14, Session Minutes, St. John's Presbyterian Church, Port Morien, 1870-1927, 20 September 1911, 132-33.

22. *PW*, 14 August 1915, 27 September 1919.

23. Ibid., 2 August 1913.

24. *Presbyterian Record*, December 1906, 525. The debate over single or communal cups also wracked the Methodist church. See O'Brien, "The Lord's Supper: Traditional Cup of Unity or Innovative Cups of Individuality,"*Methodist History*, 79-98.

25. Mervyn MacAulay to author, 11 September 1994; Carmichael et al., *History of Boularderie Presbyterian Congregation*, 8.

26. Lavery, 60.

27. Laughlin,"The Pewter Communion Services of the Presbyterian Historical Society,"*Journal of Presbyterian History*, 81.

28. In his book, *Whitebread Protestants*, Daniel Sack explores the theological battle in 19th-century North America over the use of wine and the common cup. He argues persuasively that the "obsession with health and purity" changed both the practice and theology of the sacrament. The individual cup, he asserts,"has fostered an individualistic understanding of Communion. Afraid of contamination by others in church, whitebread Protestants have shifted their theology of the sacrament, focusing on the Communion of the individual and God rather than the Communion of the entire church." See Sack, 57. Schmidt's arguments run closely parallel to those of Sack. He concludes that the transition from the common cup to individual glasses symbolized a profound paradigmatic shift in the meaning and purpose of the sacrament. He writes: "Where Victorians discerned contagion, their forebears had discovered community; where modern Christians wanted safe distance, their early modern predecessors had sought intimate sharing. The small, individual glasses were ready symbols of the diminished communal power of the sacrament."See Schmidt (2nd edition) 205.

29. MCA, PC-1002#14, Session Minutes, St. John's Presbyterian Church, Port Morien, 1870-1927, 2 April 1911, 131; Mervyn MacAulay to author, 11 September 1994.

30. Murray, *The Scotsburn Congregation, Pictou County, Nova Scotia*, 82. One of the anecdotes recounted in this book vividly illustrates the resilience of the precenting tradition in many Presbyterian churches. Murray relates an episode that occurred during one Communion Season Monday at the Earltown Presbyterian Church during the late 1850s. He describes how the young members of the congregation, emboldened by their "musical proficiency" acquired at a local singing school, started to harmonize like a choir. Their challenge to all "notions of propriety in the worship of God" did not go unremarked. The congregation was aghast and stopped singing. The precentors quickly registered their outrage that "the leadership" had been "taken out of their hands." The clergyman added to the tension of the moment with his stern words: "You have killed my soul. I can't preach here today." After delivering those lines, he strode out of the church. See 82-83.

31. MacLean, *The Presbyterian Church in North Sydney*, 7.

32. BIA, MG 13 135 (A), Meetings of the Session, East Lake Ainslie Presbyterian Church 1899-1936, entry for 27 September 1905.

33. MacDonald, *Macdonald and Mackinnon Families* (A Biographical Sketch), 27-28.

34. MacKenzie, "The Precentor," 89.

35. Cumming et al., 118.

36. MCA, PC-305#3, Session Minutes, West Bay 1898-1959, 26 June 1915.

37. Mervyn MacAulay to author, 11 September 1994. It should be noted that Carmichael's booklet, *History of Boularderie Presbyterian Congregation*, cites 1932 as the terminal date for Boularderie's outdoor communion. The traditional long communion, even after it was relocated indoors, continued to be celebrated in Boularderie until 1942.

38. *PW*, 10 September 1853.

39. MacMillan, "Book B," 60.

40. Ibid., 60.

41. Ibid., 59.

42. Grant, "Cape Breton Past and Present," *The Canadian Magazine*, vol. 7, 1901, 441.

43. Warner, 129.

44. *PW*, 23 September 1876.

45. Farnham, 625.

46. *The Blue Banner*, June 1904, n.p.

47. *MacTalla*, 13 September 1901. According to Charles W. Dunn, the liquor seller was apprehended and fined $50 by a local magistrate. See Dunn, 100; Morrison, "The Early Scotch Settlers of Cape Breton" *The Blue Banner*, May 1904, n.p.

48. *PW*, 17 August 1889.

49. Typescript account of "Sacrament Week" in Baddeck.

50. Pringle, 58.

51. Leigh Schmidt claims that sexual license and impious behaviour were the bane of 18th-century communion seasons. See Schmidt, (1st edition) 124. However, it should be noted that extant Session records for Cape Breton are silent on the issue of sexual impropriety during open-air communions.

52. McQueen, *Memory is My Diary*, 48.

53. Pringle, 58.

54. Interview, Alfred McKay, Militia Point, 23 May 1995.

55. Interview, Betty Fownes, Baddeck, 24 May 1995.

56. Dunn, 120.

57. Morrison, "The Early Scottish Settlers," n.p.; North Highlands Museum (henceforth NHM) Typescript of letter from Rev. John Murray, c. 1910; PW, 20 August 1910.

58. Farnham, 620.

59. Interview, Whitman Gillis, Blues Mills, 25 September 1995. Local residents frequently decried the physical and moral transformation of those who had sojourned in the United States. It was a common refrain that the young women who went there "changed in their ways and their speech" and became "exclusively stylish." See Hawkins, 59.

60. MacGregor, *Days that I Remember*, 26.

61. Pringle, 59.

62. Morrison, "The Early Scottish Settlers," n.p. He states that sacrament week "became the time for fashion introduction and the donning of style."

63. Interview, Flora MacMillan, Catalone, 3 September 1994.

64. Thornhill and MacDonald, 119.

65. Private source, Baddeck, 24 May 1995.

66. MCA, PC-1006#9, Peter Clarke to Presbytery of Sydney, 8 January 1879.

67. In his memoirs, Angus H. MacLean states categorically: "The outdoor ones were much more fun." See MacLean, *God and the Devil at Seal Cove*, 49.

68. Morrison, "The Early Scottish Settlers…" no pagination.

69. *MacTalla*, 13 September 1901.

70. MacDonald, Echoes of the Past, 87.

71. Private source, Sydney, 1 September 1994.

72. MacLean, *God and the Devil at Seal Cove*, 49.

73. Dunn, 99.

74. PW, 10 November 1883, 24 November 1883; Tennyson, "Introduction," xiv, xix.

75. See Donovan, "Reflections on Cape Breton Culture" in *The Island*, 21; Hornsby, *Nineteenth-Century Cape Breton*, 144, 186-200.

76. See for example, MCA, PC-305#1, Register of Communicants, 1871-1925, West Bay.

77. *PW*, 24 November 1883, 27 January 1894.

78. "Highland Communions," The Blue Banner, June 1903, n.p.

79. *PW*, 24 August 1878.

80. Ibid., 5 October 1878.

81. Ibid.

82. Ibid., 24 August 1878.

83. Ibid., 27 April 1889, 3 August 1889; MCA, PP-300, Minutes of the Presbytery of Richmond and Victoria, 1886-1899, 9 April 1889, 104. This decision echoes the steps taken by the late 17th-century Scottish church to curtail and control communions as a popular ritual. See Westerkamp, 70-71, 73.

84. MCA, PP-300, Minutes of the Presbytery of Richmond and Victoria 1886-1899, 5 November 1889, 119.

85. PW, 3 August 1889.

86. Ibid., 7 August 1897.

87. Neville, Kinship and Pilgrimage, 41.

88. MacInnes, 214.

89. *PW*, 26 December 1874. See "La na Ceist air an Eilean Mhor" *The Blue Banner*, September 1905, n.p.

90. MCA, PC-305#3, Session Minutes, West Bay, 1898-1959, 11 April 1915, 52.

91. *PW*, 15 September 1917, 14 August 1915.

92. Ibid., 16 August 1913.

93. Interview, Catherine Ross, Blues Mills, 25 September 1995.

94. Quotation provided by Rev. Ritchie Robinson to author, 19 November 1994. This saying was passed on to Rev. Robinson by Annie MacAulay who was born in Boston in 1901. Her family moved back to the Big Woods Road in Millville, Boularderie around 1908-1909.

95. MacLean, *God and the Devil at Seal Cove*, 48.

96. MCA, PC-305#3, Session Minutes, West Bay 1898-1959, 2 July 1937, 98, and 2 July 1939, 101.

97. Murray, *History of the Presbyterian Church in Cape Breton*, 267; *PW*, 31 December 1893.

98. *PW*, 19 January 1901.

99. Murray, H*istory of the Presbyterian Church in Cape Breton*, 267.

100. Schmidt subscribes to this interpretation. His overarching explanation for the decline of the outdoor communion is the triumph of "a capitalist economy with its accompanying bourgeois ethic." In short, the individualistic ethic inherent in capitalism served as a solvent on the social bonds that were central to such communal activities as open-air communions. See Schmidt, (1st edition) 194.

101. Bennett, *Sacred Spaces and Structural Style*, 78.

102. Ibid., 84

103. *PW*, 28 August 1897. It is interesting to note that by the late 19th century, the Presbyterian Witness provided extensive coverage on the unprecedented growth in the field of church construction in Cape Breton. The newspaper stated plainly, "All over Cape Breton Island, it is quite an era of church building." Presbyterian clerics increasingly viewed the church building as a place where the benefits of spiritual grace could be obtained. "Make the House of God a place where the people will gather and come under the influence of pure gospel," enjoined the *Presbyterian Witness*. See 1 September 1900. The newspaper noted with gratification the church building initiatives in Sydney, where "As a sign of their prosperity they are both enlarging their churches, especially St. Andrew's, who are adding about one hundred sittings to their present seating capacity." The modern amenities at Strathlorne's new Presbyterian church drew an enthusiastic rave:

> This new house of God, which has been named St.
> John's Church, is a beautiful building 73 ft. by 43 ft. on a
> basement of four tiers of free stone of the best quality.

The lobby is commodious, with the session room on one hand and a vestment room on the other. The finish of the interior is a testimony to good taste—the arched roof sheathing of ash laid off in squares by heavy moldings. There is a memorial window to the Rev. John Gunn, first pastor of the congregation. This window occupies a central place in a large corresponding arch behind the pulpit. The session-room and platform and transept are nicely carpeted and the various aisles matted. The building is a credit to the contractor, Mr. Faulkner of Hopewell, and to those who were associated with him, and a credit to the congregation.

The Rev. D. Sutherland, of Gabarus, cast a somewhat covetous eye on the splendid church edifice at Leitches Creek. He remarked that it was

one of the finest churches on the island. I could not but observe the improvement on the Leitch's Creek Church and people since the ordination and induction of Mr. McQuarrie. The church is beautifully finished, and the pulpit and aisles carpeted.

See *PW*, 28 August 1897, 9 November 1895, 14 September 1889.

104. There was widespread clerical abandonment on several denominational fronts—Baptist, Methodist and Presbyterian—of traditional revivalism, as the "religion of the head" supplanted the "religion of the heart." See Rawlyk, *The Canada Fire: Radical Evangelicalism in British North America, 1775-1812*, 204. Bennett also explores this development in her book, Sacred Spaces, noting that the Methodists, in particular, felt pressured to conform to the "new importance upon dignity and decorum of worship." They were motivated, in part, by the drive for "social acceptance." As a consequence, they made a concerted effort to distance themselves "from public and vocal displays of extreme emotions." Such traditions as the "old style" camp meeting "went into decline" and the main axis of worship moved from outside to inside the church. See Bennett, 216, 262.

105. *PW*, 17 August 1889.

106. Ibid., 26 July 1884.

107. *MacTalla*, 25 August 1894.

108. Ibid., 1 September 1894.

109. Ibid., 15 August 1896.

110. Ibid., 8 September 1899.

111. See, for example, MCA, Box PP-1000, Minutes of Cape Breton Presbytery, 1875-1896, vol 2, 31 January 1883, 214. The temperance movement became a driving force of social change in Cape Breton, gaining momentum as organizations sprang up around the island. The cause figured prominently in *MacTalla*, where the editor gave almost "equal space" to his commentaries on Gaelic and *stuamachd* (sobriety). See Lamond, "A Gaelic Perspective on the Temperance Movement in Nineteenth-Century Nova Scotia," 3, 5.

112. *PW*, 7 November 1885; *The Maritime Presbyterian*, 15 November 1885, 319.

113. Ibid. A similar response was elicited from the Presbytery of Inverness. See MCA, Box PP 301, Records of the Presbytery of Inverness, 1899-1917, 30-31.

114. *PW*, 21 September 1901.

115. Rita H. Farrell, *Our Mountains and Glens: The History of River Denys, Big Brook and Lime Hill (North Side), Cape Breton, Nova Scotia*, 301-2.

116. MCA, Minutes of Session, Orangedale 1912-1915, 20 February 1915, 10-11; Latimer, n.p.

117. Lavery, 22.

118. This phenomenon is skillfully dissected in Bonnie L. Hoskins, "Public Celebrations in Victorian Saint John and Halifax," PhD diss. Dalhousie University, 1991.

119. *The Home and Foreign Record*, March 1869, 71; MCA, Box PP-1000, Minutes of the Cape Breton Presbytery, vol 1, 13 May 1867, 30; *PW*, 14 December 1895, 12 October 1895, 21 May 1904. In May 1904, Dr. M. Chisholm of Halifax remonstrated against the lack of Gaelic instruction at the Theological College. This deficiency, he claimed, deprived students, many of whom would go into Gaelic congregations, of "the treasures of their vernacular." See also *MacTalla*, 2 May 1896, and *Sydney Record*, 31 March 1913.

120. Pronounced language differences created a substantial gulf within the Presbyterian Church. This situation was exemplified by the Rev. Robert Burns's decision in 1844 to omit Cape Breton from his Maritime tour. He pleaded "want of time" and "want of Gaelic." See K. Donovan, 21. There is no doubt that a high degree of competency in Gaelic was an essential skill for any Presbyterian cleric working in Cape Breton. The Rev. John Stewart, who ministered chiefly at West Bay, learned this lesson early in his career in Cape Breton. Although

he had "some knowledge" of the language in Scotland, he realized that "his usefulness as a minister" in Cape Breton "depended chiefly on his Gaelic." This proved a powerful incentive to hone his Gaelic preaching skills. See *PW*, 29 January 1898. In 1895, the Presbytery of Inverness drew public attention to the "great need of more Gaelic ministers." See PW, 14 December 1896. In February 1903, *The Blue Banner* raised the alarum in this way: "Men strong in Gaelic are much needed in this Island."

121. *PW*, 26 June 1858.

122. Ibid.

123. Ibid.

124. *MacTalla*, 2 May 1896.

125. It is interesting to note that some late-19th-century organizations in Cape Breton acknowledged and accommodated the linguistic preferences of their older Gaelic-speaking members. The minutes of the Malagawatch Auxiliary of the Woman's Missionary Society for August 1897 stated the following: "As several of the older ladies would prefer, and more readily understand, the Gaelic language, the Vice-President explained to these ladies in that language, the object of the meetings. Members were to be at liberty to ask questions in English and Gaelic, at any of the meetings, regarding the doings and objects of the Society. At any of the meetings which these ladies attended, a chapter of the Scriptures was to be read in Gaelic." See MacKinnon, *The History of the Presbyterian Church in Cape Breton*, 64.

126. *PW*, 26 December 1874; One journalist writing for Toronto's Week in June 1885 was struck by the irony of clergymen preaching in a language foreign to their parishioners. See Elliott, 25.

127. *MacTalla*, 23 September 1894.

128. "Rev. David Drummond," *The Blue Banner* (October 1904), n.p.

129. Despite the fact that Cape Bretoners figured so prominently as champions of Gaelic, *The Blue Banner* did not take up the cause. This Presbyterian monthly, which ran from 1903 to 1907, claimed as its chief mission to represent the interests of the Presbyterian church in Cape Breton. Nevertheless, during its four-year lifespan the periodical featured a paltry number of articles in Gaelic (no more than seven) and remained mute on the issue of the Gaelic lectureship. This situation is all the more surprising given that Jonathan G. MacKinnon, editor of *MacTalla* from 1892 to 1904, served as *The Blue Banner*'s business manager for a period of time. One wonders why MacKinnon's views about the linguistic revitalization of Gaelic did not spill into *The Blue Banner*.

130. PW, 9 March 1907.

131. *Ibid.*, 27 April 1907. *Eileanach* even suggested that many Gaelic-speaking clergy believed that a ministry to Gaelic speakers not only dashed their career prospects in terms of development and promotion, but ghettoized them as "incapables" in congregations which were notoriously "inadequate" and "irregular" in their payment of salaries. See *PW*, 9 March 1907, 6 April 1907. There is little doubt that the average workload for a Gaelic-speaking cleric was a heavy one. For example, the typical Sabbath schedule for the Rev. Kenneth MacKenzie, a Presbyterian minister at Baddeck for thirty-seven years, consisted of five services: Gaelic and English morning services at Baddeck; Gaelic and English afternoon services at Baddeck Forks; and an English evening service in Baddeck. See "Rev. Kenneth MacKenzie," *The Blue Banner*, (December, 1904) n.p. Even the Rev. James MacGregor, whose spiritual drive was boundless, found himself buckling under the added burden of dividing his time between the two languages. In his memoirs, he confessed that the July 1788 open-air communion had been "chiefly" delayed because he "thought it too heavy a burden first to converse with the candidates one by one, and then go through the customary services in both languages." In fact, his reluctance grew with the dread that the sacrament would become a "*Very, Very* Long Communion." Quoted in Rawlyk, 195.

132. *PW*, 27 April 1907, 25 May 1907.

133. Ibid.

134. Ibid., 1 June 1907.

135. Ibid. In his letter to the editor, J. A. McLellan made the following aside in Gaelic: "*Tha a Ghailig a falbh agus is duilich leame e.*" This statement can be roughly translated as "The Gaelic is disappearing and I am sorry about it." McLellan's comments about the attrition of Gaelic language in St. Ann's are interesting, especially in light of the fact that the infamous Norman McLeod was such a staunch defender of its use. According to *The Blue Banner*, McLeod was "never known to lead a prayer in English. If he noted one in the congregation who had only English, there would be an address in English for that one's sake, but the prayers were always in Gaelic." See "Paul-like Characteristics of the Apostle of St. Ann's," *The Blue Banner*, (June, 1903) n.p.

136. William Ross took particular umbrage at the statement that the "Gaelic preaching tends to make Highlanders poor." He defended the inherent moral and spiritual richness of this idiom, noting "The

writer had the privilege of hearing eloquent men mighty in the Scriptures on '*Lathe na Ceist*,' at open air communions where one would feel that Gaelic preaching instead of tending to make men poor made them rich and happy in this life, and heirs to the life to come." Ibid., 8 June 1907.

137. Ibid., 22 June 1907.

138. Ibid., 25 May 1907. In his letter to the *PW* of 7 December 1907, Ross estimated that there were no fewer than thirty Gaelic-speaking students at Dalhousie University, who spoke and wrote Gaelic "grammatically."

139. Ibid,. 7 December 1907.

140. Ibid., 22 June 1907. The Sydney Presbytery did offer some tangible support to the cause. In August 1907, it established two bursaries, "Hugh MacLeod Bursary" and "Matthew Wilson Bursary," the former designated specifically for a Gaelic-speaking theological student and the latter for an English-speaking theological student. See *The Blue Banner* (August 1907), n.p.

141. John Lorne Campbell, *Songs Remembered in Exile*. Aberdeen: Aberdeen University Press, 1990, 27-28.

142. Ibid., 27ff. Cape Breton Gaelic-speakers found it a real challenge to retain their language when they immigrated to the United States. The fate of Gaelic at the Scotch Presbyterian Church in Boston is a telling example of language loss. For almost fourteen years, starting around 1888, this church instituted a weekly Gaelic Sabbath service. By 1902, this tradition was sharply curtailed to a monthly Gaelic service and a weekly Gaelic prayer meeting. See PW, 8 February 1902. See also Michael Newton,"'Becoming Cold-hearted like the Gentiles Around Them': Scottish Gaelic in the United States, 1872-1912," *e-Keloi: Journal of Interdisciplinary Scottish Studies*, 63-131.

143. MacKenzie,"The Gaelic Precentor…"89.

144. Mertz, *"No Burden to Carry": Cape Breton Pragmatics and Metapragmatics*. Mertz concludes that the role of both the Presbyterian and Catholic churches in the preservation of the Gaelic language in Cape Breton was neither clearly negative nor positive. She does, however, discern a higher rate of fluency in Protestant areas, but this phenomenon is not fully explored, save for the observation that Gaelic services continued on the North Shore into the 1940s. In fact, the ministers in that region continued the 19th-century pattern of giving equal time to both Gaelic and English. See 121, 125 and 163. Michael Kennedy argues persuasively that Presbyterian worship tended to provide a greater outlet for Gaelic cultural expression than

did Catholic religious practices. He singles out the central importance of such Presbyterian institutions as precenting and the Ceist, as well as their "rich and vigorous" Gaelic sermon tradition, as key determinants in the transmission and retention of Gaelic culture in parts of Cape Breton. He also highlights the significant impact of the Presbyterian Church's use of published Gaelic devotional literature as a contributing factor to the higher rate of Gaelic literacy among Protestants. The Catholic church, Kennedy notes, relied on Latin as its primary "ritualistic language," although Gaelic still figured prominently in Catholic sermons, prayers and confessions. Despite the Latinate bias of the divine service within the Roman Catholic Church, Kennedy does note that this emphasis was offset by "a greater tendency for the Catholic community to produce its own native clergy." He speculates that this "may have made it easier for it to find clerics who understood the local language and culture" at a time when Presbyterian communities in Cape Breton struggled, often futilely, to import Gaelic-speaking clerics. Kennedy's conclusions echo those of Mertz. He writes, "the Catholic and Protestant Churches in Cape Breton appeared equally neutral regarding the Gaelic language, providing similar opportunities for its use and generally supplying Gaelic-speaking clergy while the congregations had high numbers of Gaelic speakers." See Kennedy, Gaelic Nova Scotia: An Economic, Cultural and Social Impact Study, 123.

145. Hornsby, 152.

146. Kennedy, 74.

147. Ibid., 70, 72, 58, 118. See also Cox, "Gaelic and the Schools in Cape Breton," *Nova Scotia Historical Review*, 20-40.

148. Hornsby, 180.

149. *PW*, 23 September 1865. The religious zeal of church members was seldom dampened by the physical shortcomings of some of these early church structures. It is recorded that the original Presbyterian church at Little Narrows could not accommodate its membership, even during the winter months. Still, undeterred, many braved the inclement weather and clustered around the door and the windows, straining to hear the service. The *Presbyterian Witness* reported, "We have seen on a cold winter's day four or five hundred persons without, who could not gain admittance; and so anxious were they when the word was spoken, that some of them would remain in that position until the services of the day were ended." See *PW*, 13 December 1856.

150. Neville and Westerhoff, 4. The authors use the term "religious familialism".

151. MacPhail, 47.

152. Neville, *Kinship and Pilgrimage*,130; Neville, "Kinfolks and the Covenant: Ethnic Community among Southern Presbyterians," in Bennett, ed., *The New Ethnicity*. St. Paul: West Publishing Co., 1975, 261-62.

153. In the Highlands, the open-air communion was much more explicitly political as a critique of the landowning and ruling class. See Hunter, *The Making of the Crofting Community*, 106. According to Leigh Schmidt, sacramental gatherings had the potential for "equality and inversion"; however, more typically this tradition was a field of tension and ambiguity where gender and class lines were blurred but seldom dissolved. See Schmidt, (1st edition) 104-5.

154. Neville, "Kinfolks and the Covenant," 261.

155. *PW*, 21 August 1858; 30 July 1898.

156. *The Edinburgh Christian Instructor and Colonial Religious Register*, March 1840, 116. Presbyterian clergy, knowing that their Cape Breton audiences were particularly receptive to historical allusions to their Scottish past, frequently tapped into this vast wellspring of treasured memories. On 17 August 1882, the *Presbyterian Witness* reported that the Rev. Dr. Masson's oratory with its "rich and varied allusions to other scenes and days past and gone, in the old fatherland, powerfully affected the enraptured audience."

157. Stayer, "An Interpretation of some Ritual and Food Elements of the Brethren Love Feast," *Pennsylvania Life*, 67; Humphrey, "Small Group Festive Gatherings," *Journal of the Folklore Institute*, 191.

158. MacDonald, *Group Identity in Social Gatherings*, 181, 185, 190.

159. *A View of the Whycocomagh Congregation*, 42; Grant, 63. It should be noted that in Scotland, many of the most celebrated revivals in the annals of the Presbyterian church were associated with the communion season.

160. *PW*, 27 August 1853.

161. Ibid., 29 July 1871.

162. Ibid., 3 February 1872.

163. Ibid., 8 July 1871.

164. Private papers, Mrs. Emma MacKay, Florence, Spiritual Diary of William Jardine, August 1858. Quoted in Stanley, 140.

165. Schmidt, (1st edition) 183, 212, 216.

166. Ibid., 153, 158, 183, 212, 216.

167. NHM, Rev. John Murray (typescript, c.1910).

168. "Out door Sacrament," n.p.; Morrison, "The Early Scottish Settlers,"n.p.

169. *PW*, 14 August 1897.

170."Outdoor Sacrament,"n.p.

171. One resident of Gairloch, Pictou County, provided an apt summation of the impact of modernization on traditional Presbyterian values when he wrote:"When I was a boy I was brought up on oatmeal, porridge and the Bible. Now all I see is corn flakes and Eaton's catalogue."See Hawkins et al., 59.

172. Schmidt, (2nd edition) 203.

173."Out door Sacrament,"n.p.;"The Pre-Communion Service," n.p. One contributor to *The Blue Banner* actually hinted at the desirability of resurrecting the Ceist in its original form. He wrote,"Perhaps, too, it would be better to give the man of experience in the pew a larger place in this service than is usual … might well learn a lesson for our English services from the manner in which the 'Question' is handled in the Gaelic service." See "The Pre-Communion Service," n.p. In September 1950, August 1957 and again in August 1975, Mira Ferry held traditional celebratory religious gatherings in the open-air. In all three cases, they were commemorative re-enactments. See *Cape Breton Post*, 10 August 1957; NSARM, V/F v. 70 #16, Women's Institute, "A Brief History of Mira Gut (1745-1968)."

174. This excerpt comes from a poem entitled "The Minister's Song." It was written by the Rev. Kenneth MacLeod, a native of Hume's Rear, near Bucklaw. A member of the American Presbytery of St. Lawrence, MacLeod returned to Cape Breton around 1939 to supply a number of mission posts in Cape Breton, such as St. Ann's-Englishtown and North River and Shore. See Fergusson, 53-54.

Bibliography

Primary Sources

Maritime Conference Archives (MCA)

PP-300, Minutes of Richmond Presbytery, 1857–1864.

PP-300, Minutes of Richmond and Victoria Presbytery, 1886–1899.

PP-301, Minutes of the Inverness Presbytery, 1899–1917.

PP-1000, Minutes of Cape Breton Presbytery, 1865–1875, 1875–1896.

PP-1001, Minutes of the Sydney Presbytery, 1896–1908, 1908–1919, 1919–1923.

PP-1002, Minutes of the Sydney Presbytery, 1923–1924.

PC-300#2, Session Minutes of Margaree and Cheticamp Pastoral Charge, 1896–1924.

PC-302#1, River and Lakeside Presbyterian Church, Historical Sketch of Malagawatch WMS, 1897–1947.

PC-305#1, Register of Communicants, West Bay, 1871–1925.

PC-305#2, West Bay Session Minutes, 1907–1922.

PC-305#3, West Bay Session Minutes, 1898–1959.

PC-306#5 Black River, Minutes of Congregation, 1877–1977.

PC-308#6, Minutes of Session, Orangedale and River Denys, 1912–1915.

PC-1002#14, Port Morien, St. John's Presbyterian Church Minutes, 1870–1927.

PC-1006#15, Mira-Union Presbyterian Church Session Minutes, 1874–1884.

PC-1007#4 Cape North Session Minutes 1898-1920; Communion Roll, c.1898–1926.

PC 1017/2, St. Ann's Minute Book, 1925–1988.

PC-9000/66, Session Register of the New Annan Presbyterian Church and West New Annan United Church, 1859–1934.

F & I, Box 63, #149, Rev. Matthew Wilson's Communion Sermons, 1869–1880.

Nova Scotia Archives and Records Management (NSARM)

AR 3513-AR 3514, Ron Caplan, Recorded interview with Charlie "Holy Malcolm" MacDonald, April 1984.

MGI 1471 A, Diary of the Rev. Murdoch Stewart.

V/F v. 70 #16, Women's Institute, "A Brief History of Mira Gut (1745–1968)."

MG 1, vol 745 (Rev. George Patterson).

Beaton Institute Archives (BIA)

MG 12, 219.A, "Donald Macdonald" (typescript by Estelle Jean Worfolk), 1940.

MG13, 100, Rev. McLeod's Sermons, 1797–1877.

Session book of Boularderie Kirk Session, 1875–1904.

V/F, "Presbyterian Church and Clergy," *Cape Bretoner,* 5 April 1958.

MG13, 135(A), Meetings of the Session, Deaths, Records of Baptism, Marriages…1899–1936, East Lake Ainslie Presbyterian Church.

MG 13, 85 (microfilm) Knox Presbyterian Church, Boularderie, 1875–1904.

MG14, 158 F, "Progress of Cape Breton in 100 years," 13 September 1904.

North Highlands Museum (NHM)

Typescript of letter from Rev. John Murray, c.1910.

Private Sources

Miscellaneous papers relating to the Rev. Matthew Wilson, private papers, Mrs. E. McKay, Florence, Cape Breton

Typescript account of "Sacrament Week" in Baddeck. Provided to the author by Donald Morrison, Baddeck, 21 April 2004.

Newspapers:

The Blue Banner, 1903–1907.

Bras d'Or Gazette, 1896.

The Canadian-American Gael, vol. 1, (1944); vol. 2 (c.1948).

The Canadian Magazine, 1901.

The Cape-Breton News, 1852–1854, 1862–1863.

Cape Breton Post, 10 August 1957.

The Daily Telegraph (Saint John), 1874.

The Eastern Chronicle (New Glasgow), 1935.

The Ecclesiastical and Missionary Record of the Free Church of Nova-Scotia, 1854–1858.

The Edinburgh Christian Instructor and Colonial Religious Register, 1840.

Guardian (Halifax), 13 January 1841.

The Home and Foreign Record of the Presbyterian Church of the Lower Provinces of British North America, 1861–1875.

The Home and Foreign Missionary Record for the Church of Scotland, 1835–1857.

The Home and Foreign Missionary Record for the Free Church of Scotland, 1843–1850.

MacTalla, 1892–1904.

The Maritime Presbyterian, 1885.

The Monthly Record of the Church of Scotland 1870, 1872.

The Monthly Record of the Church of Scotland in Nova Scotia, New Brunswick and Adjoining Provinces, 1869.

The Presbyterian Record, 1895, 1896, 1906.

Presbyterian Witness, 1848–1924.

Sydney Record, 1904, 1913.

Victoria-Inverness Bulletin, 1929.

Published Reports:

The First Annual Report of the Society for the Support of Gaelic Schools with an Appendix Respecting the Present State of the Highlands and Islands of Scotland & etc. Edinburgh: Printed for the Society, 1811.

Minutes of the Fifth Synod of the Maritime Provinces of the Presbyterian Church in Canada. Halifax: Nova Scotia Printing Co., 1878.

Minutes of the Presbyterian Church of the Lower Provinces of British North America. Halifax: James Barnes, 1861, 1863, 1865, 1874.

Interviews:

Betty Fownes, Baddeck, 24 May 1995.

Whitman Gillis, Blues Mills, 25 September 1995.

Catherine MacAskill, Millville, 26 May 1995.

Kay MacDonald, Blues Mills, 25 September 1995.

Sadie MacInnis (interviewed by Shamus MacDonald), North Shore, 4 August 2005.

Dolly MacKay, Baddeck, 24 May 1995.

Annie MacLeod, Sydney, 26 May 1995.

Flora MacMillan, Catalone, 3 September 1994.

Marion MacNeil, Ainslie Glen, 5 September 1994.

Alfred McKay, Militia Point, 23 May 1995.

Jessie Morrison, Baddeck, 21 August 1994.

Martha Murray, Baddeck, 24 May 1995.

Nelena Patterson, Baddeck, 5 September 1994.

Catherine Poole, Whycocomagh, 25 September 1995.

Dorothy Pottie (interviewed by Shamus MacDonald), Glendale, River Denys Mountain, 24 July 2005.

Catherine Ross, Blues Mills, 25 September 1995.

Evelyn and Alexander Smith, Wreck Cove, January 1994.

Secondary Sources

Books:

Anon, *An Address to the Members of The Presbyterian Church of Novascotia*. Pictou: E.M. McDonald, 1847.

Anon, *The Directory for the Public Worship of God's Form of Presbyterial Church Government*. Halifax: J. Munro, 1828.

Anon, *The Lord's Supper: An Appeal to the People of the Church of Scotland in the Highlands and Islands*. Edinburgh: The Saint Andrew Press, 1968.

Anon, *A View of the Whycocomagh Congregation*. N.p. 1956.

Beaton, Donald, *Some Noted Ministers of the Northern Highlands*. Inverness: Northern Counties Newspaper and Printing and Publishing Co., Ltd., 1929.

Bennett, Vicki, *Sacred Spaces and Structural Style*. Ottawa: University of Ottawa Press, 1997.

Bowman, F., *Communion Tokens of the Presbyterian Church in Canada*. Toronto: Canadian Numismatic Association, 1965.

Bridge, Donald and David Phypers, *The Meal that Unites?* London: Hodder and Stoughton, 1981.

Burnet, George S. *The Holy Communion in the Reformed Church of Scotland, 1560-1960*. Edinburgh: Oliver & Boyd, 1960.

Burns, Robert F. *The Life and Times of the Rev. Robert Burns, DD.* Toronto: James Campbell & Son, 1873.

Burns, Thomas, *Old Scottish Communion Plate.* Edinburgh: R & R Clark, 1892.

Cairns, David et al., *The Holy Communion: A Symposium.* London: SCM, 1947

Calder, William, *Communion Memories: The Seven Sayings of the Cross.* Halifax: Nova Scotia Printing Co., 1894.

Campbell, Malcolm, *Cape Breton Worthies.* Sydney: Don Mackinnon, 1913.

Cameron, James M., *Enduring Trust: First Presbyterian Church, New Glasgow, Nova Scotia, 1786-1986.* New Glasgow: s.n., 1986.

Cameron, James M., and Geo. D. Macdougall, eds., *One Hundred and Fifty Years in the Life of The First Presbyterian Church (1786-1936) New Glasgow, Nova Scotia.* Toronto: Presbyterian Publishers, 1939.

Campbell, Donald, and R. A. MacLean, *Beyond the Atlantic Roar: A Study of Nova Scotian Scots.* Toronto: McClelland & Stewart Ltd., 1974.

Campbell, Edward A., ed., *The Little Church by the Lake: A History of the Alexander Grant Memorial United Church.* N.p. n.d.

Campbell, John Lorne, *Songs Remembered in Exile.* Aberdeen: Aberdeen University Press, 1990.

Carmichael, Isabel et al., *History of Boularderie Presbyterian Congregation.* N.p. 1972.

Cumming, Peter et al., *The Story of Framboise.* Framboise: St. Andrew's Presbyterian Church, 1984.

Drummond, Andrew L., and James Bulloch, *The Church in Victorian Scotland, 1843-1874.* Edinburgh: The Saint Andrew Press, 1975.

Dunn, Charles. *Highland Settler: A Portrait of the Scottish Gael in Cape Breton and Eastern Nova Scotia.* Toronto: University of Toronto Press, 1968 (reprint).

Easthouse, Katherine, *Settlers of Southside: St. George's Channel, Nova Scotia.* N.p., 1975.

Edgar, Andrew, *Old Church Life in Scotland.* Paisley: Alexander Gardner, 1885.

Farrell, Rita H., *Our Mountains and Glens: The History of River Denys, Big Brook and Lime Hill (North Side), Cape Breton, Nova Scotia.* Truro, NS: R. Heuser Farrell, 1993.

Ferguson, Wilma et al., *Pride in the Past, Faith in the Future: A History of the Stewart United Church, 1893-1993.* Pictou: Advocate Printing &

Publishing Co. Ltd., 1993.

Fergusson, Donald A., *Beyond the Hebrides: including the Cape Breton Collection.* Halifax: Lawson Graphics Atlantic Ltd., 1977.

Gunn, Adam and John MacKay, eds., *Sutherland and Reay Country.* Glasgow: John MacKay "Celtic Monthly" Office, 1897.

Hawkins, Marjorie et al., *Gairloch, Pictou County, Nova Scotia.* N.p., 1977.

Henderson, G. D., *The Scottish Ruling Elders.* London: James Clarke & Co., Ltd., 1935.

Henderson, Ian, *Scotland: Kirk and People.* Edinburgh: Lutterworth Press, 1969.

Hornsby, S., *Nineteenth-Century Cape Breton: A Historical Geography.* Montreal: McGill-Queen's Press, 1992.

Hoskins, Bonnie L., "Public Celebrations in Victorian Saint John and Halifax," PhD diss. Dalhousie University, 1991.

Hunter, James Hunter, *The Making of the Crofting Community.* Edinburgh: John Donald Publishers, Ltd., 1976.

Hyde, Susan and Michael Bird, *Hallowed Timbers: The Wooden Churches of Cape Breton.* Erin, Ontario: Boston Mills Press, 1995.

Kennedy, John, *The Days of the Fathers in Ross-shire.* Pictou: James Paterson, 1867.

Kennedy, Michael, *Gaelic Nova Scotia: An Economic, Cultural and Social Impact Study.* Halifax: Nova Scotia Museum, 2002.

Latimer, Robert S., *Local History of Orangedale and Surrounding Area.* N.p., 1957, (reprinted in 1990).

Lavery, George, *A History of the United Church at Marion Bridge, Cape Breton.* Sydney: Lynk Printing Office, 1971.

Lavery, Mary, and George Lavery, *Tides and Times: Life on the Cape Breton Coast at Gabarus and Vicinity, 1713-1990.* N.p., 1991.

MacDermid, Alexander, *The Awakening on the North Shore, Victoria County in the 1870s.* Sydney: Lynk Printing Services, n.d.

MacDermid, Gordon E., The Religious and Ecclesiastical Life of the Northwest Highlands, 1750-1843. Ph.D. thesis, University of Aberdeen, 1967.

MacDonald, D., *Cape North and Vicinity.* N.p., 1933.

MacDonald, Donalda, *Echoes of the Past* [project funded by Careers, Cape Breton, Cape Breton Development Corporation), n.d.

MacDonald, Hugh N., *Macdonald and Mackinnon Families (A Biographical Sketch),* N.p., 1937.

MacDonald, James R., Cultural Retention and Adaptation among the Highland Scots of Carolina. Ph.D. thesis, University of Edinburgh, 1992.

MacDonald, K. Social and Religious Life in the Highlands. Edinburgh: R.W. Hunter, 1902

MacDonald, Martha Jane, *Group Identity in Social Gatherings: Tradition and Community on the Iona Peninsula.* MA thesis, Memorial University of Newfoundland, 1986.

MacFarlane, Norman, *The "Men" of The Lews.* Stornoway: The Gazette Office, 1924.

MacGregor, Francis, *Days that I Remember.* Windsor: Lancelot Press, 1976.

MacInnes, John, *The Evangelical Movement in the Highlands of Scotland, 1688 to 1800.* Aberdeen: The University Press, 1951.

Mackay, John, *The Church in the Highlands.* London: Hodder & Stoughton, 1914.

MacKinnon, A. D. *The History of the Presbyterian Church in Cape Breton.* Antigonish: Formac, 1975.

MacKinnon, Angus M., *Highland Minister.* Sydney: Catalone Press, 1997.

MacLaren, George. *The Pictou Book.* New Glasgow: The Hector Publishing Co., Ltd., 1954.

Maclean, Alexander, *The Story of the Kirk in Nova Scotia.* Pictou: Pictou Advocate, 1911.

MacLean, Angus H., *God and the Devil at Seal Cove.* Halifax: Petheric Press, 1976.

MacLean, Angus H., *The Galloping Gospel.* Boston: Beacon Press, 1966.

MacLean, Randolph D. *The Presbyterian Church in North Sydney.* Sydney Mines: Princess Printing, 1992.

MacLennan, G. A. *The Story of the Old Time Communion Service and Worship.* Toronto: The Charlton Press, 1991 (reprint, 1924).

MacLeod, A.M., *History of St. Columba Church.* N.p., 1933.

MacLeod, Dan Alex et al., *Country Roads: History of Mira.* N.p., n.d.

MacLeod, Donald, *Memoir of Norman MacLeod, DD.* London: Hodder and Stoughton, 1981.

MacLeod, John, *Scottish Theology, in Relation to Church History since the Reformation.* Edinburgh: The Publications Committee of the Free Church of Scotland, 1943.

MacMillan, Donald N., *The Kirk in Glengarry*. Finch, Ont.: D. N. MacMillan, 1984.

MacMillan, Keith and Pat MacMillan, eds., *Reminiscences of the Reverend Alexander Ross* (Private printing), 1988.

MacPhail, Margaret, *Loch Bras D'Or*. Windsor: Lancelot Press, 1970.

MacRae, Alexander, *Revivals in the Highlands and Islands in the 19th Century*. Stirling: Eneas Mackay, 1906.

McLauchlan, R. W., *Canadian Communion Tokens*. Montreal: Illiam Drysdale and Co., 1891.

McMillan, D., *The History of Presbyterianism in Cape Breton*. Sydney: Sydney Printing Co., Ltd., 1904.

McNeil, John T., *The Presbyterian Church in Canada, 1875-1925*. Toronto: General Board, Presbyterian Church in Canada, 1925.

McQueen, Angus, *Memory is My Diary*. Vol. 1, Hantsport: Lancelot Press, 1992.

Mertz, Elizabeth E., *"No burden to Carry": Cape Breton Pragmatics and Metapragmatics*. Ph.D. thesis, Duke University, 1982.

Mullan, David G., *Scottish Puritanism, 1590-1638*. New York: Oxford University Press, 2000.

Murray, John, T*he History of the Presbyterian Church in Cape Breton*. Truro: News Publishing Company, 1921.

Murray, John, *The Scotsburn Congregation, Pictou County, Nova Scotia*. Truro: News Publishing Co. Ltd, 1925.

Murray, John, *The Great Mira Parish of 1850...A Chapter in the History of the Presbyterian Church in Cape Breton*. Sydney: Don Mackinnon, 1925.

Neville, Gwen, *Kinship and Pilgrimage: Rituals of Reunion in American Protestant Culture*. Oxford: Oxford University Press, 1987.

Neville, Gwen and J. H. Westerhoff, *Learning through Liturgy*. New York: The Seabury Press, 1978.

Nicholson, John A. et al., *Middle River*. Sydney: City Printers Ltd., 1985.

Noll, Mark A. et al., eds., *Evangelicalism: Comparative Studies of Popular Protestantism in North America, the British Isles, and Beyond, 1700-1900*. Oxford: Oxford University Press, 1994.

Patterson, George, *Memoir of the Rev. James MacGregor, DD*. Philadelphia: Joseph M. Wilson, 1859.

Perrot, Philippe, *Fashioning the Bourgeoisie*. Princeton: Princeton University Press, 1994.

Phillips, Alastair, *My Uncle George: The Respectful Recollections of a Backslider in a Highland Manse.* Glasgow: George Outram and Co., Ltd, 1954.

Pringle, Will, *Pringle's Mountain.* Windsor: Lancelot Press, 1976.

Rawlyk, G.A., *The Canada Fire: Radical Evangelicalism in British North America, 1775-1812.* Montreal: McGill-Queen's University Press, 1994.

Ross, James, *An Address to The Members of The Presbyterian Church of Nova Scotia.* Pictou: E.M. McDonald, 1847.

Rutherford, Jane MacKay, *I came from Pictou County: The Recollections of Jane MacKay.* Rutherford. Regina: F.L. Dunbar, 1984.

Sack, Daniel, *Whitebread Protestants: Food and Religion in American Culture.* New York: St. Martin's Press, 2000.

Schmidt, Leigh, *Holy Fairs: Scottish Communions and American Revivals in the Early Modern Period.* Princeton: Princeton University Press, 1989.

Schmidt, Leigh, *Holy Fairs: Scotland and the Making of American Revivalism.* (revised edition) Grand Rapids, Michigan: William B. Eerdman's Publishing Company, 2001.

Scobie, Charles H. H. and G. A. Rawlyk, eds., *The Contribution of Presbyterianism to the Maritime Provinces of Canada.* Montreal & Kingston: McGill-Queen's University Press, 1997.

Shiells, R., *The Story of the Token.* Philadelphia: The Presbyterian Board of Publication and Sabbath-School Work, 1902.

Smith, Dennis and H. E. Taussig, *Many Tables: The Eucharist in the New Testament and Liturgy Today.* London: SCM Press, 1990.

Stanley, Laurie, *The Well-Watered Garden: The Presbyterian Church in Cape Breton, 1798-1860.* Sydney: UCCB Press, 1983.

Tennyson, Brian, ed., *Impressions of Cape Breton.* Sydney: UCCB Press, 1986.

Thornhill, Bonnie and W. James MacDonald, eds., *The Road to Tarbot.* Sydney: City Printers, 2004.

Vernon, C.W. *Cape Breton, Canada.* Toronto: Nation Publishing Co., 1903.

Warner, Charles D., *Baddeck and that Sort of Thing.* Boston: James R. Osgood and Co., 1874.

Watson, James, and Ellison Robertson, eds., *Sealladh Gu Taobh.* UCCB Art Gallery, Sydney, 1987.

Westercamp, Marilyn J., *The Triumph of Laity: Scots-Irish Piety and the Great Awakening, 1625-1760.* Oxford: Oxford University Press, 1980.

Wood, Ruth Kedzie, *The Tourist's Maritime Provinces.* New York: Dodd, Mead and Co., 1915.

Wright, David F., David C. Lachman & Donald E. Meek, eds., *Dictionary of Scottish Church History & Theology.* Edinburgh: T. and T. Clark Ltd., 1993.

Articles:

Archibald, Mrs. Charles, "Early Scottish Settlers in Cape Breton," *Collections of the Nova Scotia Historical Society,* vol. 18 (1914), 69-101.

Beaton, D., "Fast Day and Friday Fellowship Meeting Controversy in the Synod of Sutherland and Caithness (1737-1758)," *Transactions of the Gaelic Society of Inverness,* vol. 29 (1914–1919), 159-82.

Burns, Robert, "The Holy Fair," quoted on http://eir.library.utoronto.ca/rpo/display/poem329.html (accessed 21 July 2005).

Bruce, Steve, "Social Change and Collective Behaviour: the Revival in Eighteenth Century Ross-shire," *The British Journal of Sociology,* vol. 34, no. 4 (1983), 554-72.

Bynum, William B., "'The Genuine Presbyterian Whine': Presbyterian Worship in the Eighteenth Century," *American Presbyterians* vol. 74, no. 3 (1996), 157-70.

Caplan, Ron, "Gaelic Precenting on the North Shore," *Cape Breton's Magazine,* vol. 27, 45-49.

Caplan, Ron, "Hattie Carmichael of the Meadow Road," *Cape Breton's Magazine,* no. 35, 1-10.

Clarke, Alison, "'Days of Heaven on Earth': Presbyterian Communion Seasons in Nineteenth-Century Otago," *Journal of Religious History,* vol. 26, no. 3 (October 2003), 274-97.

Clements, William M., "The Physical Layout of the Methodist Camp Meeting," *Pioneer America,* vol. 5, no. 1 (1973), 9-15.

Cooley, Steven D., "Manna and the Manual: Sacramental and Instructive Constructions of the Victorian Methodist Camp Meeting during the mid-Nineteenth Century," *Religion and American Culture,* vol. 6, no. 2 (1996), 131-59.

Cox, Lori, "Gaelic and the Schools in Cape Breton," *Nova Scotia Historical Review,* 14 (1994), 20-40.

Donovan, Kenneth Donovan, "Reflections on Cape Breton Culture," in *The Island: New Perspectives on Cape Breton History, 1713-1990,* edited by Kenneth Donovan, Sydney: UCCB Press, 1990, 1-28.

Elliott, Shirley B., "A Nineteenth Century Tourist in Cape Breton," *Journal of Education,* Part II (Summer, 1971), 24-26.

Farnham, C. H., "Cape Breton Folk," *Harper's New Monthly Magazine*, vol 72, (1885/1886), 607-25 [Reprinted in *Acadiensis*, vol. 8, no. 2, (Spring, 1979), 90-106, intro by Stephen F. Spencer, 90-106].

Grant, John Webster, "Brands from Blazing Heather: Canadian Religious Revival in the Highland Tradition," *The Canadian Society of Presbyterian History Papers*, 1991, 59-74.

Guildford, Janet, "The Role of Women in the Urban Middle Class Household Economy, Halifax, Nova Scotia, 1840–1880," (paper presented to the Canadian Historical Association meeting, Calgary, July 1994)

Humphrey, Linda T., "Small Group Festive Gatherings," *Journal of the Folklore Institute*, vol. 16, (1979), 190-201.

Hunter, A. Mitchell, "The Celebration of Communion in Scotland since the Reformation," *Records of the Scottish Church History Society*, vol. 3 (1929), 161-73.

Innes, Alexander T., "The Religion of the Highlands," *The British and Foreign Evangelical Review*, vol. 21 (July, 1872), 413-46; 73-105.

Johnston, John, "'Ticket to Heaven': The Rise and Fall of the Communion Token," *The Canadian Society of Presbyterian Historical Society Papers*, (1986), 15-21.

Lamond, Mary J., "A Gaelic Perspective on the Temperance Movement in Nineteenth-Century Nova Scotia," undergraduate essay, St. Francis Xavier University, March 1995.

Laughlin, Ledlie I., "The Pewter Communion Services of the Presbyterian Historical Society," *Journal of Presbyterian History*, vol. 44 (June 1955), 83-88.

MacInnes, Dan, "The Culture of Consideration: A Commentary on Gaelic Cultural Survival," *New Maritimes*, vol. 7, no. 6 (July-August 1989), 20-21.

MacInnes, John, "The Origin and Early Development of the 'Men'," *Records of the Scottish Church History Society*, vol. 8 (1942), 16-41.

MacLeod, Norman, "Putting on the Kilt: The Scottish Stereotype and Ethnic Community Survival in Cape Breton," *Canadian Ethnic Studies*, vol. 20, no. 3 (1988), 132-46.

Masson, Rev. Dr., "The Gael in the Far West," *Transactions of the Gaelic Society of Inverness*, vols. 3 & 4 (1873–1875), 26-44.

Meek, Donald E., "Evangelicalism and Emigration: Aspects of the Role of Dissenting evangelicalism in Highland Emigration to Canada," in *Proceedings of the First North American Congress of Celtic Studies* (Ottawa, 1988), 15-25.

Morrison, M. D.,"Religion in old Cape Breton,"*Dalhousie Review,* vol. 20 (1940), 181-96.

Neville, Gwen,"Kinfolks and Covenants: Ethnic Community among Southern Presbyterians,"in John W. Bennett, ed., *The New Ethnicity: Perspectives from Ethnology.* St. Paul: West Publishing Co., 1975, 93-109.

Newton, Michael,"'Becoming Cold-hearted like the Gentiles Around Them': Scottish Gaelic in the United States, 1872-1912," *E-Keltoi: Journal of Interdisciplinary Scottish Studies,* vol. 2, (2003), 63-131.

O'Brien, Betty A., "The Lord's Supper: Traditional Cup of Unity or Innovative Cups of Individuality," *Methodist History,* vol. 32, no. 2 (1994), 79-98.

Owen, Trefor M.,"The 'Communion Season' and Presbyterians in a Hebridean Community," *Gwerin,* vol. 1, (1956), 53-66.

Parman, Susan, "Orduighean: A Dominant Symbol in the Free Church of the Scottish Highlands," *American Anthropologist,* vol. 92 (1990), 295-305.

Ramsay, David A., and R. Craig Koedel,"The Communion Season— An 18th Century Model," *Journal of Presbyterian History,* vol. 54 (1976), 203-16.

Schmidt, Leigh Eric, "'A Church-going People are a Dress-loving People': Clothes, Communication, and Religious Culture in Early America," *Church History,* vol. 58 no 1, (March 1989), 36-51.

Smith, Matthew, "Distinguishing Marks of the Spirit of God: Eighteenth-Century Revivals in Scotland and New England": Available from www.star.ac.uk STAR (Scotland's Transatlantic Relations) Project Archives, April 2004. [accessed 21 July 2005].

Smout, T. C.,"Born Again at Cambuslang: New Evidence on Popular Religion and Literacy in Eighteenth-Century Scotland," *Past and Present,* no. 97 (November, 1982), 114-27.

Stayer, Jonathan, "An Interpretation of some Ritual and Food Elements of the Brethren Love Feast," *Pennsylvania Life,* vol. 34 (1984-85), 61-70.

Vickery, Edgar J.,"Communion tokens," *Collections of the Royal Nova Scotia Historical Society,* vol. 24 (1938), 155-73.

Websites

http://edinburghguide.com/edgeforum   [EdinburghGuide.com— Celtic Connections News, 21 January 2005: accessed 15 July 2005]

http://www.materialreligion.org/ [Material History of American Religion History Project: accessed 15 July 2005]

Index